Just 24 Days Till Christmas

Other Books by MyLinda Butterworth

For Health's Sake: A Cancer Survivor's Cookbook

Frogazoom with Linda S. Day

The Monster Run

Storytelling CD
Just So Wild: Animal Stories from Around the World

Just 24 Days Till Christmas

compiled and written by

MyLinda Butterworth

Day to Day Enterprises ❋ *Oviedo, Florida*

Just 24 Days Till Christmas
© 1997, 1998, 2007 MyLinda Butterworth

Illustrations on pages 10, 11, 18, 28, 29, 40-42, 63,64, 75, 98, 102, 109, 116-118, 153-155, 159-161 by Linda S. Day ©1997

Paperback:
ISBN-13:   978-1-890905-10-1
ISBN-10:   1-890905-10-0
Hardcover:
ISBN-13:   978-1-890905-54-5
ISBN-10:   1-890905-54-2

Printed in the United States of America
10 9 8 7 6 5 4

Revised in 1998 & 2007

Library of Congress Catalog Card Number 97-077079

Published by Day to Day Enterprises • Oviedo, FL
Visit us on the web at http://www.daytodayenterprises.com

This book is dedicated to my family, and all those special angels who help us remember why we celebrate this joyous holiday ... Christmas!

Table of Contents

Preface

Christmas is a wonderful time of year. It is a time when we feel good-will towards all men. When we feel the blessings of giving. And the childlike joy of seeing presents under the tree. It is also a time of hustle, bustle and continual frustration that there is not enough time to do everything we want to do. A time when we want to do something different but can't think of anything new to do. We want to establish family traditions, but don't know where to start.

This book was compiled to help you create new family traditions and provides stories, activities and recipes that everyone young and old can enjoy. Take the time to sit down by yourself or with your children each day and read the stories in this book. Select an activity to celebrate the season or a recipe that might cause you to remember a special Christmas in your past. Create your own Christmas memories and traditions and write them down (don't forget the photos too). A calendar has been included so that you might write down what special thing you did each day. Write down what recipes you liked and would want to continue to use each year. I have included recipes for one complete meal each week, so that you will think about slowing down enough to enjoy a good meal with the ones you love. Record the stories that touched your heart or ones that you remember growing up with. By doing this you create a history of this Christmas that becomes a record for generations to come.

This holiday above all others has a special place in my heart, for it is truly the season of love. You can feel and smell it in the air. You can see it in the smiles on peoples faces. There is something special about Christmas. As a child we didn't have the money to spend on lots of gifts and so I spent my youth making the majority of my gifts for family and friends. Many of the activities in this book are related to that idea of making your own gifts. You may note that under the title of the activity it will state that this project is good for gift giving,, take advantage of it. For it is in the giving that we find true happiness. Also you will find that I have added notes that relate to how something may have been used in my family. It is my way of showing you that Christmas is a collection of memories of sight, smell, sound and feelings.

It is my sincere hope that you will slow down enough to enjoy the season, create some memories and some traditions. And that if by some chance I have been able to help you do that, then I am truly grateful. Look beyond the commercialism of this holiday to the true reason for the season and count your blessing. Now take a deep breath and go out there and have a Very Merry Christmas!

Special Thanks

I would like to thank my mother, Linda S. Day for the many hours she spent helping me fix the instructions for my activities and for all the many illustrations she provided for this book. I know I could not have completed this book without her.

Special thanks to my father, Robert O. Day who always said that I could do anything I put my mind to, and never stopped believing in me.

I am extremely thankful to my husband, Mike who believed in this project. For his patience in dealing with a messy house and extra child care responsibilities during the final month of production.

To my children, Nicole and Sean who patiently waited for mommy to finish her book. Knowing that when it was done, we would be able to spend lots more time playing again.

To the following individuals who helped me with the kitchen testing of all the recipes. We had a great deal of fun testing and tasting all of the foods that were prepared. Without their help I would not have been able to perfect the instructions and variations. Thank you to: The Potter Family (Lisa, Rick, Jeremy, Thomas and Erin); Bob and Linda Day; Kathy Roti; The Grigley Family (Roland, Laurie, Rebecca, Ashley, Erin and Laila); The Allen Family (Bret, Brenda, Whitney and Kailie); Paula Kalinoski and Koko Mihilas.

DECEMBER

Sunday	Monday	Tuesday	Wednesday	Thursday	Friday	Saturday

Jest 'Fore Christmas

Eugene Field

Father calls me William, sister calls me Will,
Mother calls me Willie, but the fellers call me Bill!
Mighty glad I ain't a girl—ruther be a boy,
Without them sashes, curls, an' things, that's worn by Fauntleroy!
Love to chawnk green apples an' go swimmin' in the lake—
Hate to take the castor-ile they give for belly-ache!
'Most all the time, the whole year round, there ain't no flies on me,
But jest 'fore Christmas I'm as good as I kin be!

Got a yeller dog named Sport, sick him on the cat;
First thing she knows she doesn't know where she is at!
Got a clipper sled, an' when us kids goes out to slide,
'Long comes the grocery cart, an' we all hook a ride!
But sometimes when the grocery man is worrited an' cross,
He reaches at us with his whip, and' larrups up his hoss,
An' then I laff an' holler, "Oh, ye never teched *me*!"
But jest 'fore Christmas I'm as good as I kin be!

Gran'ma says she hopes that when I git to be a man,
I'll be a missionarer like her oldest brother, Dan,
As was et up by the cannibuls that live in Ceylon's Isle,
Where every prospeck pleases, an' only man is vile!
But gran'ma she has never been to see a Wild West show,
Nor read the life of Daniel Boone, or else I guess she'd know
That Buff'lo Bill an' cow-boys is good enough for me!
Excep' jest 'fore Christmas, when I'm good as I kin be!

And then old Sport he hangs around, so solemn-like an' still,
His eyes they seem a-sayin': "What's the matter, little Bill?"
The old cat sneaks down off her perch an' wonders what's become
Of them two enemies of hern that used to make things hum!
But I am so perlite an' 'tend so earnestly to biz,
That mother says to father: "How improved our Willie is!"
But father, havin' been a boy hisself, suspicions me
When, jest 'fore Christmas, I'm as good as I kin be!

For Christmas, with its lots an' lots of candies, cakes, an' toys,
Was made, they say, for proper kids, an' not for naughty boys:
So wash yer face an' bresh yer hair, an' mind yer p's and q's,
An' don't bust out yer pantaloons, and don't wear out yer shoes;
Say "Yessum" to the ladies, an' "Yessur" to the men,
An' when they's company, don't pass yer plate for pie again;
But, thinkin' of the things yer'd like to see upon the tree,
Jest 'fore Christmas be as good as yer kin be!

Sweet Smelling Christmas Cards
Art Project

MATERIALS LIST:

scissors	*white glue*
glitter	*small bowls*
gelatin (any flavor)	*water*
paintbrushes or cotton swabs	*permanent markers or*
index weight paper	*rubber stamps*
ruler	*envelopes*

INSTRUCTIONS:

1. Measure the size of your envelopes to determine what size card you want to make.

2. Cut card ¼ inch smaller than the envelope, so that it will fit inside the envelope. For instance if your envelope is 7½ x 5 inches then you should cut your card 7 ¼ x 4¾ inches folded dimensions (actual size of card before folding is 7¼ x 913½ inches).

3. Score card down the center and fold in half, so that you will know where to place the design.

4. Lay paper flat on table and draw a design on front of card (i.e.; star, bell, tree, etc. (If you think your artistic abilities are lacking try tracing around cookie cutters for your design)) with a permanent marker. If you use a water color marker the color will run when you begin painting, although this may be a desirable effect. You may also rubber stamp a design on the front of your card or outline paint with colored white glue for different effect.

5. Dissolve 3 tablespoons of gelatin with 1 tablespoon of water. This should be a thick paintable consistency, if it is too thick then add a little more water. I like to make several different colors.

6. Now paint your design with one gelatin mix at a time, using either a paintbrush or cotton swabs. Little fingers will work well with cotton swabs, you can put one in each color and then throw them away when you are done.

7. Let card set overnight.

8. Write a simple message inside the card with permanent pen and sign. Now paint over the message with glue and dust with glitter.

9. When they are all dry, fold them up and stuff them into the envelope. Mail or deliver to friends and family. What a sweet treat for the nose.

VARIATION: For an embossed look to your card write/draw your message or design in white glue. Let dry completely. Then paint over glue with flavored paint.

VARIATIONS: Follow the same process for making your own gift tags and thank-you notes. You can also use gelatins that are not as aromatic and add a drop of cinnamon oil for a seasonal scent.

These cards smell yummy when you take them out of the envelope and they colors are great too!

Cracker Candy

This recipe is cheap, easy, and great. Tastes like toffee."
Lisa Potter - Kitchen Tester

1   cup butter
1   cup sugar
    saltine crackers
1   6 ounce bag chocolate chips

Place butter and sugar into a medium sized pot. Bring butter and sugar to a boil and boil one minute.

Lay saltine crackers in single layer on lightly greased cookie sheet covering bottom completely. Pour sugar mixture over crackers and bake in preheated oven at 400° for 5 minutes. Take out of oven and pour 1 bag of chocolate chips over and quickly spread melting chocolate over entire surface of crackers. Put in fridge/freezer and chill until set. When set, remove from pan and break into desired size pieces and serve.

VARIATION 1: Try any variety of chips on the cracker candy. For instance; semi-sweet chocolate, milk chocolate, mint chocolate, peanut butter or maybe even butterscotch. Then when you have finished spreading out the melting chocolate you may want to sprinkle some fancy sugars or decorations on it just for fun.

VARIATION 2: Replace the saltine crackers with graham crackers. Follow directions listed above. After you spread chocolate over crackers sprinkle with finely chopped pecans. AWESOME!

A Lump of Coal for Christmas
Robert O. Day

One of the stories that my mother, Hope Stauffer Day, would tell from time to time as Christmas approached, was one about her childhood. Mom was one of four children growing up on a farm in Willard, Utah sometime early in the 1920's. Farm life was hard, money was scarce and treats of any nature were hard to come by.

For these reasons, Christmas was always looked forward to. Everyone knew that they would receive a gift of some kind. Sometimes it was an orange, sometimes a homemade toy, sometimes - if fall harvest had been good and there was a little money set aside - there might even be a store bought item like a scarf, a handkerchief or a rubber ball.

One year as Christmas was approaching, each of the children hung up a stocking on a nail that had been partially pounded into the rough wooden mantle over the fireplace. There was no Christmas tree in the house, but there were brightly colored paper chains hung around the house and crayon colored Christmas pictures hanging on most walls.

All of the children were trying very hard to be good, except, little Hope, my mother. She had wanted a new doll, as her old rag doll had finally wore out, and she told her mother dozens of time a day she just had to have a new doll. [What she wanted was a doll from the store, but she was willing to settle for a homemade one.] Grandmother finally got tired of telling Mom to be patient and that she couldn't promise her anything. She also told her that if she didn't be quiet about it that all she would get for Christmas was a lump of coal in her stocking. That calmed Mom down for a day or two, but on Christmas Eve she started in again whining about having to have a doll.

The whole matter was finally solved when her father overheard Hope's whining. He told her in no uncertain terms that as far as he was concerned all she deserved was a lump of coal and to go to bed!

As Mom told it, "I didn't sleep much that night, waiting to get my doll to play with. I knew my father loved me and he really didn't mean what he said. That would be too mean and he was not a mean man, at least I hoped he wasn't. Finally I drifted off to sleep."

"Morning came early, as it always did on the farm. There were chores to do and breakfast to be prepared, just like any other day of the week." I jumped out of my nice warm bed and hurried to get into my clothes

before I froze. The old farm house didn't have heat anywhere except the kitchen where the stove was, and in the living room fireplace, which was only lighted on Sundays and special occasions.

"Everyone hurried through their morning chores before they dared go into the living room to peek at the stocking's hanging on the fireplace. Finally chores were finished, breakfast was over and the dishes were done and put away. It was time to get the socks." Quickly we ran into the cold living room and took our sock off of our nail and returned to the warm kitchen. There at the table we each took our turn removing the hidden treasure from our sock, starting with the youngest. Lee pulled a small wooden horse with wheels on the bottom from his sock, and a small candy cane. Everyone voiced their approval and told him how lucky he was to have such a toy.

"Then Afton removed a small hand carved bowl and spoon that she could use to pretend to feed her doll. She also had a candy cane and again there was voiced approval. Glen found a small bag of marbles and a candy cane, then it was my turn.

"Carefully I reached into my sock and felt something very hard. Was it the head of the store bought doll I wanted, could I be so lucky? I felt ashamed that I had whined and complained so much to my mother, but I could hardly wait to get the small doll out and see its face. All eyes were on me as I removed a **large lump of coal** from my stocking. I couldn't believe it, I didn't dare breathe and I didn't know what to say. There in my coal dust covered hand was a black lump of coal. No doll, no candy cane, just coal." Then to make things worse, my brothers and sisters began to laugh.

"I threw the piece of coal into the coal bucket, ran out of the room and up the stairs to my cold bedroom. For what seemed an eternity I sat in the cold with my mind racing over the events of that last few days and the many warnings that I had received. How could I have been so foolish? Instinctively I fell to my knees beside my bed and began to offer a very sobbing prayer to Heavenly Father. I poured out my heart in repentance and promised to be good if only I could have another chance.

"Just then I heard my mother's voice calling from downstairs. Jumping up, I quickly dried my eyes on the bed quilt, wiped my nose on the underpart of my slip, and walked slowly through the doorway and down the steps. There in the nice warm kitchen sat my mother and father, waiting for me. My brothers and sister were busy playing in the corner

with their toys as I walked toward my mother, with my eyes still looking at the floor. I told them how sorry I was and promised that next year I would be different.

"My father, with a teasing sound in his voice, asked if I wanted to wait that long? He said, "repentance had its own reward and that if I would carefully sweep the kitchen floor, all would be forgiven." "Slowly and carefully I swept the floor, not wishing to miss a thing. I had swept everywhere but under the table, and as my broom reached under the long table cloth I felt it strike something next to the leg. I lifted up the table cloth and as I bent over to look under the table to see what it was, I couldn't believe my eyes. There, leaning against the leg of the table sat a rag doll with a big smile on its face. She was clothed in a blue dress covered by a red apron with a large pocket, and in that pocket was a candy cane."

Mother never said if she had remembered to finish sweeping the floor, but she did say that every Christmas for the rest of her life she remembered that long ago time, when at a special time of year, she learned of the blessings of repentance and the undying love of her parents.

LINDA DAY ©19—

Handsy Reindeer T-shirt
Art Project/Wearable Art

MATERIALS LIST:

T-shirt
brown Acrylic Paint
textile Medium
1 inch paint brush
2 large wiggly eyes
1 large red pom pom
fabric glue
cardboard insert
wax Paper
masking tape
foam Plate
newspaper
wet paper towels to wash up with

INSTRUCTIONS:

1. Pre-wash t-shirt to remove sizing or recycle an existing shirt for this project.

2. Tape wax paper to one side of cardboard form. The form should be cut to the body size of the shirt.

3. Place cardboard form inside of T-shirt with wax paper surface facing front of shirt, where you intend to paint.

4. Secure shirt around cardboard with masking tape.

5. Place newspaper and foam plate on table with brush to paint your hands and feet. Mix equal amounts of medium and paint.

6. Using paintbrush, paint the bottom of one foot, cover evenly. Place T-shirt on floor and center foot (toes up please) in middle of T-shirt. Now do what your mother never let you do to your clothes, step down hard and leave your dirty footprint in the middle of your shirt. This becomes the head of the reindeer with your toes becoming his curly hair. NOW WASH YOUR FOOT!

7. Now that your foot is clean, make sure that there is plenty of paint left on the plate and place your hands one at a time in the paint. Check to see that they are evenly covered in paint, if you have too much paint on your hands blot them lightly on newspaper. Spread your fingers wide and carefully place your hands on either side of his head to make the antlers. Apply equal pressure to make a good imprint, but don't move them. Lift them straight up to avoid smearing.

8. Let dry overnight.

9. Using a good fabric glue attach wiggly eyes and red pom pom for nose (if you wanted you could just paint a big red shiny nose). Let dry.

Note: Could add a bow and jingle bells at neck. Use your own imagination to decorate your reindeer. Perhaps you want to add lights that twinkle (kits are available at your local craft store).

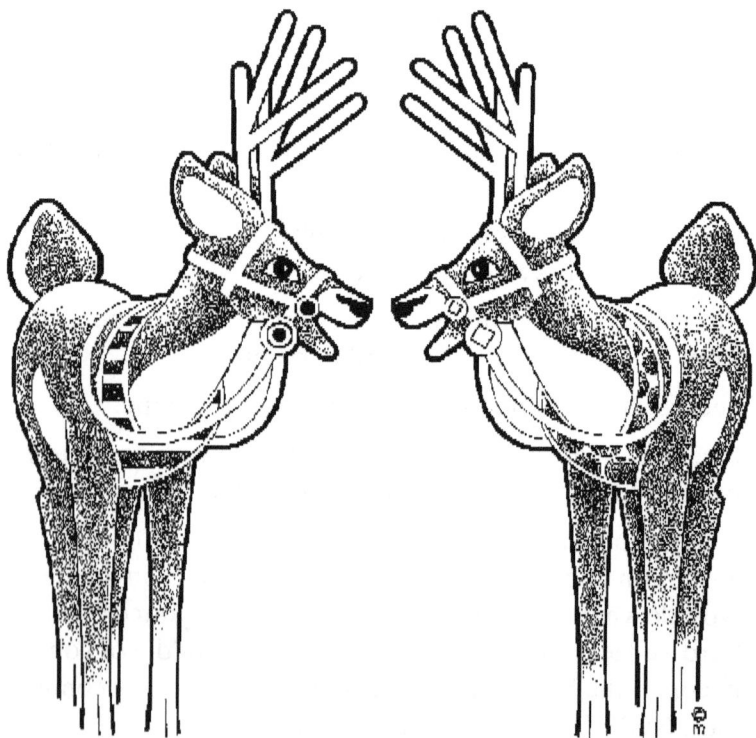

Grandma Va's Fudge

Bring on the fudge. MMMMMM!!!! Bret Allen-Food Taster

3   (6 oz.) packages of chocolate chips
1   (7 oz) jar marshmallow cream
1   cup butter
2   cups nuts (pecans or walnuts)
2   teaspoon vanilla
4½ cups sugar
1   large can evaporated milk

In a large bowl mix the chocolate chips, marshmallow cream, butter, nuts and vanilla and set aside.

In a large pot (if the pot is not big enough the sugar mix may boil over*) mix sugar and milk till sugar dissolves. Boil sugar and milk exactly 9 minutes after it comes to a boil. Remove from heat and pour over other ingredients. Mix well and pour into one 9x13 and one 8x8 inch, buttered pan. Let set in refrigerator until firm enough to cut. It stays soft.

Makes about 120 one inch squares of fudge or 4-5 pounds

GIFT SUGGESTION: I find this recipe makes a lot of fudge. So I like to line metal tins with wax paper and pour the fudge directly into the tins. When it is set up, I trim away the extra wax paper, place a plastic knife tied with a ribbon on top and place the lid on it. This way when it is all done it is ready for gift giving. Even better make the boxes on day 18 and line the bottoms with colored plastic wrap and fill each box with fudge, I call this fudge for one.

NOTE: According to Grandma's notes this is the See's Fudge recipe. I don't know if this is true or not ... you be the judge. I always thought it was a cross between a soft fudge and divinity. It is truly my family's favorite. No Christmas is complete without this fudge.

* I do the majority of my candy making in my electric wok. The sides are angled and I can keep a constant temperature for making perfect candy.

A Sweet Reminder

MyLinda Butterworth

My mother's family settled in Indiana when they arrived from the old country and with them came many glorious stories. But it was a story that my Great Grandma Pearl always told me around Christmas that has stayed with me for a lifetime. I'm sure that you have heard it too, for it is a story of a man's desire to give people sweet reminders of the **reason for the season** of Christmas.

It was Christmas time and my world was covered in a blanket of newly fallen snow. Everywhere windows were adorned with garlands of holly and berries of red, Christmas trees were laden with beautiful decorations, and people were smiling even under their heavy coats and arms full of parcels. Yes, it's Christmas! A wonderful time of year, a time when we forget about ourselves and remember our friends, neighbors and those who are less fortunate than we are. I was nearly twelve and it seemed to me there had to be more to this holiday than bright tinsel and packages under a tree.

My father was a candy maker by trade, so of course, Christmas was a very busy time of year in his candy shop, especially the week before the great event. When everyone else was out sledding, I was busy helping Papa make truffles, or toffee, or waiting on customers, so I got very little time to play with my friends. Not that I minded, but there were other things I would rather be doing than spending all my time stuck in the candy shop.

One evening after the door had been latched and the closed sign hung in place, I went to the back of the shop to walk home with Papa for dinner. He was standing at one of the marble tables with his head down.

"Papa, what's wrong?" I asked.

Without looking up he beckoned to me, "Come here Hannah." As I reached his side, he looked up and asked, "Do you know why we celebrate Christmas?"

"Sure, everyone knows that!" I said, with a big smirk on my face, "It is the day when Kris Kringle brings presents to all the good little boys and girls, and the day when Jesus was born. Right?" I asked, half cocky and half questioning.

Papa took my face in his hands and looked deep into my eyes, for what seemed an eternity and quietly, yet firmly said, "Hannah, the birth of the Savior is the **only** reason for Christmas. Kris Kringle was a game we played with you when you were young to help you to be good. On Christmas Eve when you put your shoes out to see whether you received a present or a lump of coal, that was all part of the game. But don't you remember our reading the story of Jesus' birth every Christmas morning before we opened any presents?"

I did of course and shook my head to acknowledge the fact. Papa is a very religious man and my whole family had been raised to be the same. I should have been a little more careful with my answer, but as usual I spoke before I thought about it.

I could tell that something was really bothering my Papa. Something that went much deeper than the fact that I didn't take his question seriously. "Papa, what's bothering you? Did I say something wrong? If I did I'm sorry, I didn't mean it. I ...". But before I could finish my sentence, Papa put his arms around me and gave me a big hug, "My little one," he said excitedly, "how could I have been so blind? It is not you that has done anything wrong, but you who has given me an idea!"

Then Papa took me by the shoulders and gave me a little shake, his eyes were twinkling with excitement and then he danced me around the kitchen until I was dizzy with the spinning. "I know what to do," he shouted, " I know what to do! I will make a special candy. It will only be available during Christmas time! What do you think Hannah? Do you think it will work?"

My head was still spinning and my eyes were just beginning to focus again, but I understood what my Papa was getting at. "Yes!" I exclaimed, "It's a wonderful idea, but ... what kind of candy will it be and how will it help people remember what Christmas is all about?"

My Papa stopped and said thoughtfully, "I don't know, but I am sure once I've eaten your mother's fine dinner tonight and talked with the rest of the family it will come to me. Let's go home!" And with that we put on our coats, hats and mittens, and arm and arm we walked, no, I would say we nearly floated home.

When we reached home, mother as usual had the table set and the food waiting and ready for us to sit and eat. After grace had been said, I attacked the food on the table. I was simply ravenous since I missed lunch, due to the shop being so busy. The evening meal was always the highlight of my day, because the whole family was together at one time and we got to share whatever was on our minds and relate the events of the day. Tonight my head was reeling after my talk with Papa in the shop, and I was anxious for him to bring up the subject of the special Christmas candy. Mother was about to clear the dishes from the table, when Papa asked her to sit down. "Tonight, family," Papa began and everyone cringed because such a statement usually meant someone was in trouble, "Hannah and I were discussing the meaning of Christmas. We decided a special Christmas candy needed to be created that will help people remember that Christmas is about Christ's birth, not presents, or Kris Kringle, or music, or friends, or any of those things but simply the Saviors birth. Will you help me come up with some ideas for my new candy creation?" With that the room was suddenly a buzz with an abundance of suggestions, filling the air with excitement, and there at the end of the table was Papa smiling with great contentment.

I don't remember half of the ideas that flowed across the dinner table that evening, but there were some good ones that Papa said he would think about. My younger brother Hans said it should be a candy that lasts a long time and my sister Evette suggested that it should be in the shape of a "J" for Jesus. Christian, age three, thought it should be shaped like a baby just like him at which the whole family burst into laughter. After about an hour of discussion, Papa announced that his brain could hold no more suggestions and recommended we all help mother clean up from dinner and retire for the evening.

It was hard to go to sleep that night with so many things floating around my head, and I wondered what Papa was going to do. I knew that when he said his evening prayers he would ask God to help him, and being the kind of man my Papa was, God would surely help him find the answer .

The next morning I arose as usual to the smell of bread baking in the oven and sausage sizzling in the pan. I dressed myself for the day and headed downstairs for breakfast. When I arrived at the table, mother told me that Papa had left for the candy shop at daybreak and wanted me to hurry along when I was ready because he would need my help again today. Normally I would have tried to beg off, saying that Evette could go today, but I knew that Papa would be busy creating a special Christmas treat and I wanted to be there when it was finished. I gulped down my food, kissed my mother and ran out the door, forgetting all my outside winter clothes. It only took one step into the cold crisp morning air to remind me that I needed all those winter trappings or be ready to turn into an icicle.

I ran all the way to the candy shop, not stopping to slide across the frozen creek as I usually did, or even throw snowballs at the cats in the street. I knew that today was going to be special and I didn't want to miss a thing. When I reached the back door of the shop, I could smell the familiar scent of peppermint in the air. I loved peppermint, and wondered what kind of candy Papa was making this morning. I tossed my hat, coat, scarf and mittens on the rack and scurried over to where Papa was busily shaping candy on the cold marble. I threw my arms around him, planted a big kiss on his check, and said, "Good Morning Papa, any special candy visions during the night?" He simply smiled and said, "Yes! Would you like to see it?"

I thought to myself what kind of silly question is that to ask me after sending me to bed with my mind reeling with visions of sweet confections dancing in my head. "Of course I do, show me quick."

"First close your eyes and open your mouth." I quickly closed my eyes and opened my mouth and Papa placed a small piece of candy in my mouth. The taste was peppermint but the consistency was hard. I let the candy dissolve in my mouth and it was not only tasty, but refreshing. When I opened my eyes Papa stepped aside and I saw a whole table of white and red striped candy, formed in the shape of a J. I threw my arms around my Papa, knowing that he had truly been inspired by our Maker, and gave him a great big bear hug. "It is wonderful," I exclaimed, "surely it will be everything you want it to be."

Papa pinched my check and winked at me, "I couldn't have done it without you. For it was you that inspired me to want to shout to the people in the streets that Jesus's birth is the reason we celebrate Christmas. Now I can let my candy creation shout it for me. Help me display them in the window and make a sign for our latest candy the 'Christmas Candy Cane'."

As it turned out, my father's candy was a success, not just in our little town in Indiana, but all over the world. People may not always remember the reason he made it, or what it symbolizes. I know that some people see his creation as simply the candy cane, a colorful, meaningless decoration that is edible. But every Christmas when Papa puts up his "Christmas Candy Cane" sign, he always explains the symbolism. It reads:

The Christmas Candy Cane

Christmas is a season that we all celebrate. I want to add my witness to the celebration. So I created this simple confection. Each part of the candy represents something special.

The pure white candy represents the virgin birth and sinless nature of Christ.

The hardness of the candy represents the solid rock on which His church is founded.

The small red stripes represent the scourging Jesus received by which we are healed.

The large red stripes are for the blood shed by the Savior for us all.

The candy is shaped in the form of the letter "J" to denote the precious name of Jesus.

I hope this special Christmas Candy will help us remember why we are celebrating this time of year.

Many Thanks .... Jules

Each year at Christmas I buy candy canes. Some are used as decorations and some are gobbled up by my family. But at least once each year I remember the story that my Great Grandmother Pearl told me about the creation of the candy cane and the reason for its existence. I don't know if the story is true, but the candy and its legend are part of my life. Perhaps now that you have heard this tale it will cause you to reflect on the **reason for the season** in a different way too.

Candy Cane Mice
Art Project/Decoration/Gift Idea

MATERIALS LIST:

candy cane
2 plastic wiggly eyes
red pom pom
yarn scraps
felt square
scissors
white glue
copy of pattern

INSTRUCTIONS:

1. Trace or photocopy the pattern.

2. Cut out of felt the body (A) and ears (B) of mouse.

3. Carefully cut on the dotted lines in body (A) to make slits for ears.

4. Insert ears (B) through the slits you cut in A, and fluff out the ears.

5. Glue on wiggly eyes.

6. Glue on two pieces of yarn cut 2 inches long each at tip of nose area. Glue red pom pom over yarn to create a nose with whiskers.

7. Insert candy cane under the body of mouse and between the ears and the body leaving crooked end extending out of the back for the mouse's tail.

Note: These adorable candy cane mice are so easy to make that you won't need a lick of help! Make a box full and give them as presents or us them as party favors or place cards on the table. They are great fun to make and you can make them in a multitude of colors.

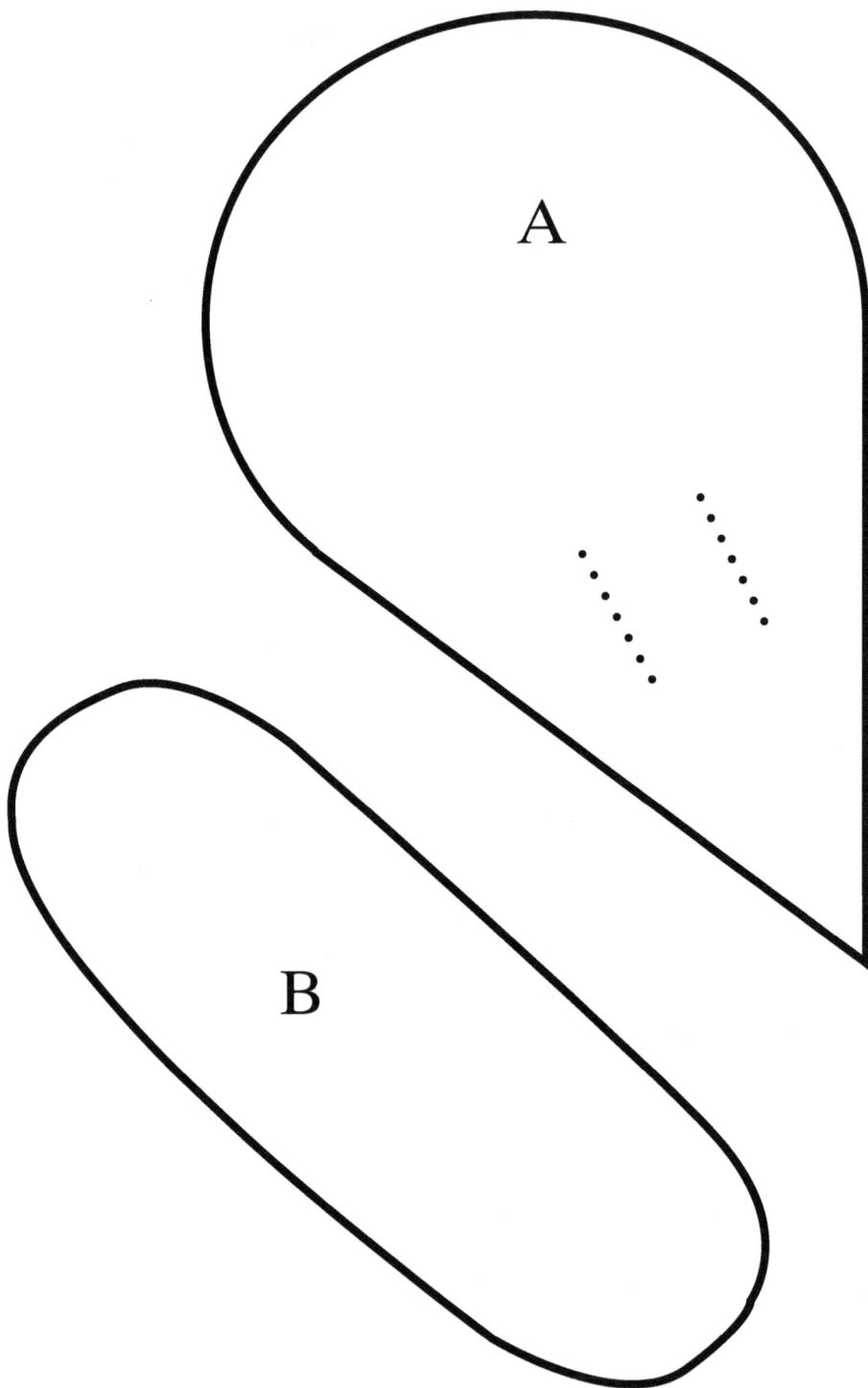

A

B

Winter-Mint Crunch

1   6 ounce package white chocolate chips
6-8   candy canes (crushed)

Melt white chocolate according to your favorite method. Mix chocolate until smooth. Add crushed candy canes and mix well. Line a cookie sheet with wax paper. Pour melted chocolate mix on to wax paper and spread out until thin and it covers entire surface. Place cookie sheet in freezer for a few minutes or until chocolate is set. Remove from freezer and break into desired pieces. (This mix may also be molded if candy canes are broken into small enough pieces).

Makes about 1/2 pound

Tiger Butter

1   6 ounce package semi-sweet or milk chocolate chips
1   6 ounce package peanut butter chips

In separate bowls melt the chocolates according to your favorite method. Mix chocolate until smooth. Line a cookie sheet with wax paper. Smooth chocolate over entire surface of wax paper. Then drop random dots of melted peanut butter chips on top of the chocolate. Swirl two flavors together with a knife to marbleize (don't overdue). When you are finished, lightly tap the pan on the counter. This causes the chocolate to smooth out, place pan in freezer. Leave in freezer for a few minutes or until chocolate is set or refrigerate 1 hour or until firm. Break into pieces.

Makes about 1 pound

The Legend of the Snow Maiden

An old Russian Folk Tale
as told by MyLinda Butterworth

A very long time ago, in the forests of Russia, there lived a peasant named Ivan and his wife, Maria. Although they had many friends and loved each other very much, they were saddened because they had no children of their own. More than anything in the world, they wanted a son or a daughter to share their love with, to laugh and play with. One winter day, they stood watching some children in the forest having a wonderful time romping and playing in the snow. They watched as they built snowmen and as they made and threw snowballs at one another. Suddenly Ivan turned to his wife and said, "Maria, the children look like they are having such fun making a snowman, why don't we make one of our own?" So Ivan and Maria went out into the forest and began making a person out of snow.

Maria then said, "Ivan, since we have no children of our own, let us make a snow girl." Ivan agreed, and they proceeded to craft a pretty little maiden out of snow. They rolled and patted the snow into dainty little hands and feet, then they gave their little snow maiden braids and little eyes and a petite nose and mouth. When they were finished, they thought that she was the prettiest little girl that they had ever seen. Overcome by their creation. Ivan said, "Little snow maiden, speak to me," and Maria chimed in, "Yes, won't you please come to life so you can play with the other children!" As they gazed at their little snow girl they noticed that her eyes began to flutter and her cheeks began to glow a rosy color. At first they thought they were imagining things and Maria rubbed her eyes and looked again to behold charming little girl standing before them, where only a few moments ago their snow maiden had stood. In amazement Ivan finally said, "Where do you come from child? Who are you?"

"I have come from the land of winter. From the land of snow and ice and cold," the child replied. "I am come to be your daughter, your own little girl." With that the little girl ran and threw her arms around the couple and hugged them, and all three of them wept for joy. When the tears ended, they all began to talk at once and laughter followed their excitement, for this was the happiest day of their lives. They called to all of their neighbors in the nearby huts and introduce them to their beautiful little girl. Everyone stayed up late that night, marveling over the miracle that had happened. There was much singing, dancing and celebrating.

All during the long winter the little snow maiden played with the other children, and her parents beamed as they beheld their little girl and thought she was the prettiest of all. Everyone loved the little snow maiden, as she was a well mannered, happy child. She would run and play with the other children all day. Ivan and Maria were very happy.

When the first signs of spring appeared, the air grew warmer, the snow started to melt, and their little snow maiden seemed to grow more tired each day. She was no longer lively and actually appeared to be unhappy.

One day she came to her parents, her eyes filled with tears and sang a little song:

"The time has come for me to go. Away up North to the land of snow."

Her mother and father begged her to stay, saying they would not allow her to leave. They became so sad they began to cry. Ivan jumped up and stood in front of the door to stop the little snow maiden from leaving while Maria grabbed her and hugged her tightly. But as Maria held her little girl, the child began to melt. Soon there was nothing left of the Snow Maiden except her white fur cap and white fur coat. There where the snow maiden once stood was only a puddle of water. Maria sank to the floor and wept, while Ivan tried to console her, but he too had tears in his eyes.

As Maria and Ivan talked about their daughter, they wondered if perhaps someday their little snow maiden might return. All summer long they were lonely. It was difficult for them to hear the children laughing for it reminded them of their little girl. Summer turned to fall and fall into winter, and once again the snow began to fall and the weather was cold and icy outside. One night as Ivan and Maria watched the snow falling gently outside their window there came a knock on the door. They wondered who could be calling at this late hour, but then they heard a familiar voice singing a song:

"Mother! Father! Open the door! The snow has brought me back once more!"

Ivan ran to the door and threw it open. There was their little snow maiden. Maria ran to her daughter and the three of them hugged and kissed, laughed and cried. All that winter she lived with them and played with the other village children. But with each spring thaw, she returned to the land of winter from whence she came, where it was always cold with ice and snow. Ivan and Maria no longer wept for their daughter for they knew that when the weather turned cold and the snow began to blanket the land that their little snow maiden would return. And so it was for the rest of their lives, that every winter the little snow maiden would return to the couple and every spring she bid them farewell.

Glitter Snow Globe
Art Activity/ Gift Idea

MATERIALS LIST:

glitter, any color
jar with a lid (baby food jars are great)
Low melt glue gun
small figurines or Christmas ornaments
plastic leaves or flowers
acrylic paint

INSTRUCTIONS:

1. Paint the lid, then set aside to dry.

2. Glue the figure and any decorations inside the lid with glue gun, making sure that you stay within the rubber seal area. Let dry completely.

3. Put water and glitter into jar.

4. Place figure into the fluid and tighten the lid. Run a bead of hot glue along outside jar edge to seal, then set aside to dry.

5. Shake gently to watch the snow fall.

NOTE: It used to be that you could buy moth flakes, and they made the best snow inside the domes. If you can find them at a hardware store use the same amount of flakes as you use glitter.

Snowball Cookies

They just melt in your mouth. " Linda Day - Kitchen Tester

2¼   cup flour
    dash of salt
1   cup butter
1   teaspoon vanilla
½   cup powdered sugar
1   cup finely chopped nuts
    additional powdered sugar for rolling

Preheat oven to 400° F. Sift flour and salt together in bowl, add nuts. Mix butter, vanilla and powdered sugar together in medium sized bowl. Add flour mixture and blend well. Chill dough for 1 hour.

With hands, roll dough into 1 inch balls. Place on ungreased cookie sheet about ½ inch apart. Bake for 10 to 12 minutes or until set but not brown. While warm, roll in powdered sugar. Cool. Roll in sugar again.

"Yes, Virginia, There Is a Santa Claus"

Francis Church

The following first appeared on the editorial page of the New York Sun on September 21, 1897, as the response to a little girl's probing question about Santa Claus.

Dear Editor:

I am 8 years old. Some of my little friends say there is no Santa Claus. Pap says "If you see it in *The Sun* it's so." Please tell me the truth. Is there a Santa Claus?

Virginia O'Hanlon,
115 West 95th Street

Virginia, your little friends are wrong. They have been affected by the skepticism of a skeptical age. They do not believe except they see. They think that nothing can be which is not comprehensible by their little minds. All minds, Virginia, whether they be men's or children's, are little. In this great universe of ours, man is a mere insect, an ant, in his intellect, as compared with the boundless world about him, as measured by the intelligence capable of grasping the whole of truth and knowledge.

Yes, Virginia, there is a Santa Claus. He exists as certainly as love and generosity and devotion exist, and you know that they abound and give to your life its highest beauty and joy. Alas! how dreary would be the world if there were no Santa Claus. It would be as dreary as if there were no Virginias. There would be no childlike faith then, no poetry, no romance to make tolerable this existence. We should have no enjoyment, except in sense and sight. The eternal light with which childhood fills the world would be extinguished.

Not believe in Santa Claus! You might as well not believe in fairies! You might get your papa to hire men to watch in all the chimneys on Christmas Eve to catch Santa Claus, but even if they did not see Santa Clause coming down, what would that prove? Nobody sees Santa Claus, but that is no sign that there is no Santa Claus. The most real things in the world are those that neither children nor men can see. Did you ever see fairies dancing on the lawn? Of course not, but that's no proof that they are not there. Nobody can conceive or imagine all the wonders there are unseen and unseeable in the world.

You may tear apart the baby's rattle and see what makes the noise inside, but there is a veil covering the unseen world which not the strongest man, nor even the united strength of all the strongest men that ever lived, could tear apart. Only faith, fancy, poetry, love, romance, can push aside that curtain and view and picture the supernal beauty and glory beyond. Is it all real? Ah, Virginia, in all this world there is nothing else real and abiding.

No Santa Claus! Thank God he lives, and he lives forever. A thousand years from now, Virginia, nay, ten times ten thousand years from now, he will continue to make glad the heart of childhood.

Dear Editor:

I am 8 years old. Some of my little friends say there is no Santa Claus. Pap says "If you see it in The Sun it's so." Please tell me the truth is there a Santa Claus?

Virginia O'Hanlon

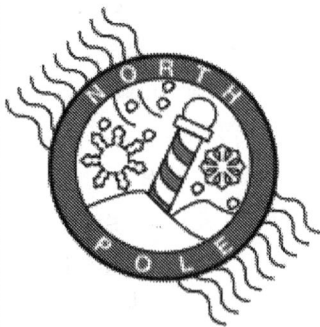

VIRGINIA O'HANLON
115 WEST 95TH STREET
NEW YORK CITY, NEW YORK

PEACE
CHRISTMAS

EDITOR
NEW YORK SUN

Down the Chimney, Santa
Art Activity/ Party Favor

MATERIALS LIST:

*markers or crayons
scissors
glue
index weight paper
copies of this page*

INSTRUCTIONS:

1. Trace or photocopy the cutouts on this page for each child.

2. Let the children color the cutouts however they like. Paste the colored pictures to a piece of heavy or index weight paper.

4. Cut out the pictures along the solid lines.

5. Fold the chimney piece along the dotted lines. Then glue the tab to the inside of the cube to hold the chimney together. Fold up the bottom tab and glue.

6. Cut slits along the dotted lines on the Santa piece as shown. Then put Santa inside the chimney with his arms on the outside.

7. Hook a sack of toys onto Santa's right hand and glue it in place. Place name on bag.

SUGGESTION: Fill the chimney with candy or a small wrapped gift and use as a party favor or a place card with their name written on the bag.

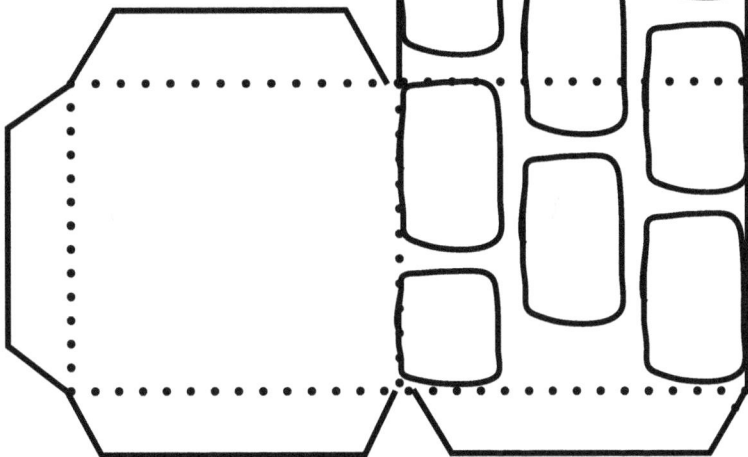

Banana Nut Bread

½ cup margarine or butter
1 cup sugar
2 eggs
1 cup mashed bananas
¼ cup milk
1 teaspoon lemon juice
2 cups flour
1½ teaspoons baking powder
½ teaspoon baking soda
1 teaspoon vanilla
¼ teaspoon salt
½ cup chopped nuts

Preheat oven to 350° F. Cream margarine and sugar. Add eggs and beat. Add bananas, milk, and lemon juice. Sift dry ingredients and add vanilla and nuts. Mix until blended. Bake in well-greased 8x4x3 inch loaf pan for 1 hour.

Makes 1 loaf

VARIATION: For variety try adding 1 cup of Bits o'Brickle chips to the batter before baking. Or to make pumpkin bread use the following: 1 cup of pumpkin for the bananas, ½ teaspoon of cinnamon and ½ teaspoon of ginger.

"Moist and tasty"

The Fir Tree

Hans Christian Anderson

O UT in the woods stood such a pretty little fir tree. It grew in a good place, where it had plenty of sun and plenty of fresh air. Around it stood many tall comrades, both fir trees and pines.

The little fir tree was in a headlong hurry to grow up. It didn't care a thing for the warm sunshine, or the fresh air, and it took no interest in the peasant children who ran about chattering when they came to pick strawberries or raspberries. Often when the children had picked their pails full, or had gathered long strings of berries threaded on straws, they would sit down to rest near the little fir. "Oh, isn't it a nice little tree," they would say. "It's the baby of the woods." The little tree didn't like their remarks at all.

Next year it shot up a long joint of new growth, and the following year another joint, still longer. You can always tell how old a fir tree is by counting the number of joints it has.

"I wish I were a grown-up tree, like my comrades," the little tree sighed. "Then I could stretch out my branches and see from my top what the world is like. The birds would make me their nesting place, and when the wind blew I could bow back and forth with all the great trees."

It took no pleasure in the sunshine, nor in the birds. The glowing clouds, that sailed overhead at sunrise and sunset, meant nothing to it.

In winter, when the snow lay sparkling on the ground, a hare would often come hopping along and jump right over the little tree. Oh, how irritating that was! That happened for two winters, but when the third winter came the tree was so tall that the hare had to turn aside and hop around it.

"Oh to grow, grow! To get older and taller," the little tree thought. "That is the most wonderful thing in this world."

In the autumn, woodcutters came and cut down a few of the largest trees. This happened every year. The young fir was no longer a baby tree, and it trembled to see how those stately great trees crashed to the ground, how their limbs were lopped off, and how lean they looked as the naked trunks were loaded into carts. It could hardly recognize the trees it had known, when the horsed pulled them out of the woods.

Where were they going? What would become of them?

In the springtime, when swallows and storks came back, the tree asked them, "Do you know where the other trees went? Have you met them?"

The swallows knew nothing about it, but the stork looked thoughtful and nodded his head. "Yes, I think I met them," he said. "On my way from Egypt I met many new ships, and some had tall, stately masts. They may well have been the trees you mean, for I remember the smell of fir. They wanted to be remembered to you."

"Oh, I wish I were old enough to travel on the sea. Please tell me what it really is, and how it looks."

"That would take to long to tell," said the stork, and off he strode.

"Rejoice in your youth," said the sunbeams. "Take pride in your growing strength and in the stir of life within you."

And the wind kissed the tree, and the dew wept over it, for the tree was young and without understanding.

When Christmas came near, many young trees were cut down. Some were not even as old or as tall as this fir tree of ours, who was in such a hurry and fret to go traveling. These young trees, which were always the handsomest ones, had their branches left on them when they were loaded on carts and the horses drew them out of the woods.

"Where can they be going?" the fir tree wondered. "They are no taller than I am. One was really much smaller than I am. And why are they allowed to keep all their branches? Where can they be going?"

"We know! We know!" the sparrows chirped. "We have been to town and peeped in the windows. We know where they are going. The greatest splendor and glory you can imagine awaits them. We've peeped through windows. We've seen them planted right in the middle of a warm room, and decked out with the most splendid things - gold apples, good gingerbread, gay toys, and many hundreds of candles."

"And then?" asked the fir tree, trembling in every twig. "And then?

What happens then?"

"We saw nothing more. And never have we seen anything that could match it."

"I wonder if I was created for such a glorious future?" The fir tree rejoiced. "Why, that is better than to cross the sea. I'm tormented with longing. Oh, if Christmas would only come! I'm just as tall and grown-up as the trees they chose last year. How I wish I were already in the cart, on my way to the warm room where there's so much splendor and glory. Then–then something even better, something still more important is bound to happen, or why should they deck me so fine? Yes, there must be something still grander! But what? Oh, how I suffer, and how I long. I don't know what's the matter with me."

"Enjoy us while your may," the air and sunlight told him. "Rejoice in the days of your youth, out here in the open."

But the tree did not rejoice at all. It just grew. It grew and was green both winter and summer–dark evergreen. People who passed it said, "There's a beautiful tree!" And when Christmas time came again they cut it down first. The ax struck deep into its marrow. The tree sighed as it fell to the ground. It felt faint with pain. Instead of the happiness it expected, the tree was sorry to leave the home where it had grown up. It knew that never again would it see its dear old comrades, the little bushes and the flowers around it—and perhaps not even the birds. The departure was anything but pleasant.

The tree did not get over it until all the trees were unloaded in the yard, and it heard a man say, "That's a splendid one. That's the tree for us." Then two servants came in fine livery, and carried the fir tree into a big splendid drawing–room. Portraits were hung all around the walls. On either side of the white porcelain stove stood great Chinese vases, with lions on the lids of them. There were easy chairs, silk-covering sofas and long tables strewn with picture books, and with toys that were worth a mint of money, or so the children said.

The fir tree was planted in a large tub filled with sand, but no one could see that it was a tub, because if was wrapped in a gay green cloth and set on a many-colored carpet. How the tree quivered! What would come next? The servants and even the young ladies helped it on with its fine decorations. From its branches they hung little nets cut out of colored paper, and each net was filled with candies. Gilded apples and walnuts hung in clusters as if they grew there, and a hundred little white, blue, and even red, candles were fastened to its twigs. Among its green branches swayed dolls that it took to be real living people, for the tree had never seen their like before. And up at its very top was set a large gold tinsel star. It was splendid, I tell you, splendid beyond words!

"Tonight," they all said, "ah, tonight how the tree will shine!"

"Oh thought the tree, "if tonight would only come! If only the candles were lit! And after that, what happens then? Will the trees come trooping out of the woods to see me? Will the sparrows flock to the windows? Shall I take root here, and stand in fine ornaments all winter and summer long?"

That was how much it knew about it. All its longing had gone to its bark and set it to aching, which is as bad for a tree as a headache is for us.

Now the candles were lighted. What dazzling splendor! What a blaze of light! The tree quivered so in every bough that a candle set one of its twigs ablaze. It hurt terribly.

"Mercy me!" cried every young lady, and the fire was quickly put out. The tree no longer dared rustle a twig–it was awful! Wouldn't it be terrible if it were to drop one of its ornaments? Its own brilliance dazzled it.

Suddenly the folding doors were thrown back, and a whole flock of children burst in as if they would overturn the tree completely. Their elders marched in after them, more sedately. For a moment, but only for a moment, the young ones were stricken speechless. Then they shouted till the rafters rang. They danced about the tree and plucked off one present after another.

"What are they up to?" the tree wondered. "What will happen next?"

As the candles burned down to the bark they were snuffed out, one by one, and then the children had permission to plunder the tree. They went about it in such earnest that the branches crackled and, if the tree had not been tied to the ceiling by the gold star at the top, it would have tumbled headlong.

The children danced about with their splendid playthings. No one looked at the tree now, except an old nurse who peered in among the branches, but this was only to make sure that not an apple or fig had been overlooked.

"Tell us a story! Tell us a story!" the children clamored, as they towed a fat little man to the tree. He sat down beneath it and said, "Here we are in the woods, and it will do the tree a lot of good to listen to our story. Mind you, I'll tell only one. Which will you have, the story of Ivedy-Avedy, or

the one about Humpty-Dumpty who tumbled downstairs, yet ascended the throne and married the Princess?"

"Ivedy-Avedy," cried some. "Humpty-Dumpty," cried the others. And there was a great hullabaloo. Only the fir tree held its peace, though it thought to itself," Am I to be left out of this? Isn't there anything I can do?" For all the fun of the evening had centered upon it, and it had played its part well.

The fat little man told them all about Humpty-Dumpty, who tumbled downstairs, yet ascended the throne and married the Princess. And the children clapped and shouted, "Tell us another one! Tell us another one!" For they wanted to hear about Ivedy-Avedy too, but after Humpty-Dumpty the story telling stopped. The fir tree stood very still as it pondered how the birds in the woods had never told it a story to equal this.

"Humpty-Dumpty tumbled downstairs, yet he married the Princess. Imagine! That must be how things happen in the world. You never can tell. Maybe I'll tumble downstairs and marry a princess too," thought the fir tree, who believed every word of the story because such a nice man had told it.

The tree looked forward to the following day, when they would deck it again with fruit and toys, candles and gold. "Tomorrow I shall not quiver," it decided. "I'll enjoy my splendor to the full. Tomorrow I shall hear about Humpty-Dumpty again, perhaps about Ivedy-Avedy too." All night long the tree stood silent as it dreamed its dreams, and the next morning the butler and the maid came in with their dusters.

"Now my splendor will be renewed," the fir tree thought. But they dragged it upstairs to the garret, and there they left it in a dark corner where no daylight ever came. "What's the meaning of this?" the tree wondered. "What am I going to do here? What stories shall I hear?" It leaned against the wall, lost in dreams. It had plenty of time for dreaming as the days and nights went by. Nobody came to the garret. And when at last someone did come, it was only to put many big boxes away in the corner. The tree was quite hidden. One might think it had been forgotten.

"It's still winter outside," the tree thought. "The earth is too hard and covered with snow for them to plant me now. I must have been put here for shelter until springtime comes. How thoughtful of them! How good people are! Only, I wish it weren't so dark here, and so very, very lonely. There's not even a little hare. It was so friendly out in the woods when the snow was on the ground and the hare came hopping along. Yes, he was friendly even when he jumped right over me, though I did not think so then. Here it's all so terribly lonely."

"Squeak, squeak!" said a little mouse just then. He crept across the floor, and another one followed him. They sniffed the fir tree, and rustled in and out among its branches.

"It is fearfully cold," one of them said. "Except for that, it would be very nice here, wouldn't it, you old fir tree?"

"I'm not at all old," said the fir tree. "Many trees are much older than I am."

"Where did you come from?" the mice asked him. "And what do you know?" They were most inquisitive creatures.

"Tell us about the most beautiful place in the world. Have you been there? Were you ever in the larder, where there are cheeses on shelves and hams that hang from the rafters? It's the place where you can dance upon tallow candles-where you can dart in thin and squeeze out fat."

"I know nothing of that place," said the tree. "But I know the woods where the sun shines and the little birds sing." Then it told them about its youth. The little mice had never heard the like of it. They listened very intently, and said, "My! How much you have seen! And how happy it must have made you."

"I?" The fir tree thought about it. "Yes, those days were rather amusing." And he went on to tell them about Christmas Eve, when it was decked out with candies and candles.

"Oh," said the little mice, "how lucky you have been, you old fir tree!"

"I am not at all old," it insisted. " I came out of the woods just this winter, and I'm really in the prime of life, though at the moment my growth is suspended."

"How nicely you tell things," said the mice. That night they came with four other mice to hear what the tree had to say. The more it talked, the more clearly it recalled things and it thought, "Those were happy times. But they may still come back–they may come back again. Humpty-Dumpty fell downstairs, and yet he married the Princess. Maybe the same thing will happen to me." It thought about a charming little birch tree that grew out in the woods. To the fir tree she was a real and lovely princess.

"Who is Humpty-Dumpty?" the mice asked it. So the fir tree told them the whole story, for it could remember it word by word. The little mice were ready to jump to the top of the tree for joy. The next night many more mice came to see the fir tree, and on Sunday two rats paid it a call, but they said that the story was not very amusing. This made the little mice so sad that they began to find it not so very interesting either.

"Is that the only story you know?" the rats asked.

"Only that one," the tree answered. "I heard it on the happiest evening of my life, but I did not know then how happy I was."

"It is a very silly story. Don't you know one that tells about bacon and candles? Can't you tell us a good larder story?"

"No," said the tree.

"Then good-by, and we won't be back," the rats said, and went away.

At last the little mice took to staying away too. The tree sighted, "Oh, wasn't it pleasant when those gay little mice sat around and listened to all that I had to say. Now that, too, is past and gone. But I will take good care to enjoy myself, once they let me out of here."

When would that be? Well, it came to pass on a morning when people came up to clean out the garret. The boxes were moved, the tree was pulled and thrown—thrown hard—on the floor. But a servant dragged it at once to the stairway, where there was daylight again.

"Now my life will start all over," the tree thought. It felt the fresh air and the first sunbeam strike it as it came out into the courtyard. This all happened so quickly and there was so much going on around it, that the tree forgot to give even a glance at itself. the courtyard adjoined a garden, where flowers were blooming. Great masses of fragrant roses hung over the picket fence. The linden trees were in blossom, and between them the swallows skimmed past, calling, "Ti-lira-lira-lee, my love's come back to me." But it was not the fir tree of whom they spoke.

"Now I shall live again," it rejoiced, and tried to stretch out its branches. Alas, they were withered, and brown, and brittle. It was tossed into a corner, among weeds and nettles. But the gold star that was still tied to its top sparkled bravely in the sunlight.

Several of the merry children, who had danced around the tree and taken such pleasure in it at Christmas, were playing in the courtyard. One of the youngest seized upon it and tore off the tinsel star.

"Look what is still hanging on that ugly old Christmas tree," the child said, and stamped upon the branches until they cracked beneath his shoes.

The tree saw the beautiful flowers blooming freshly in the garden. It saw itself, and wished that they had left it in the darkest corner of the garret. It thought of its own young days in the deep woods, and of the merry Christmas Eve, and of the little mice who had been so pleased when it told them the story of Humpty-Dumpty.

"My days are over and past," said the poor tree. "Why didn't I enjoy them while I could? Now they are gone—all gone."

A servant came and chopped the tree into little pieces. These heaped together quite high. The wood blazed beautifully under the big copper kettle, and the fir tree moaned so deeply that each groan sounded like a muffled shot. That's why the children who were playing near-by ran to make a circle around the flames, staring into the fire and crying, "Pif! Paf!" But as each groan burst from it, the tree thought of bright summer day in the woods, or a starlit winter night. It thought of Christmas Eve and thought of Humpty-Dumpty, which was the only story it ever heard and knew how to tell. And so the tree was burned completely away.

The children played on in the courtyard. The youngest child wore on his breast the gold star that had topped the tree on its happiest night of all. But that was no more, and the tree was no more, and there's no more to my story. No more, nothing more. All stories come to an end.

Brown Bag Ornaments
Art Project/Decoration

MATERIALS LIST:

> brown grocery bags
> assorted large Christmas cookie cutters
> white glue
> glitter
> scissors
> markers
> assorted decorations (lace, buttons, yarn, ribbon, etc.)
> raffia ribbon
> polyester stuffing

INSTRUCTIONS:

1. Cut apart brown paper bag so it will lay flat. Cut out two 4-6 inch squares for each ornament.

2. Place cookie cutter on paper squares. Trace around cookie cutter using your markers.

3. With your markers decorate both sides of your ornament, have fun and use your imagination.

4. Cut out design 1/2 inch larger than the marker line, don't forget to cut both pieces at the same time.

5. Turn one piece of you decoration over. Run 1/8 inch glue line around edges leaving an opening about 2 inches on one side so you can stuff it when it is dry.

6. Put the two plain sides together, with decorated sides showing. Run finger along edges to seal glue, make sure your opening does not get glued shut. Set aside to dry 15 minutes and work on another ornament.

7. Now that your ornament is dry, use small pieces of polyester stuffing and push gently into your ornament opening with a pencil or chopstick. When your ornament is puffy, glue a piece of raffia ribbon into opening to form hanger, now glue opening shut hold tightly with your finger or use a clothespin to hold till dry.

8. You are ready to finish decorating your ornament with dry flowers, ribbon, yarn, buttons, sequins, glitter, lace or whatever tickles your fancy. Now you are ready to trim the tree.

Note: You can use the new decorative scissors to cut your edges. If you want brighter colors use acrylic paints.

TREE TRIMMING PARTY

EASY CHILI • GOLDEN CORNMEAL MUFFINS
•CHRISTMAS TREE COOKIE PUZZLE •

Easy Chili

Not too spicy, very flavorful. I'd make it again."
Judy Bowden - Kitchen Tester

1	(16 oz) can dark red kidney beans, drained, rinsed
1	(16 oz) can pinto beans, drained, rinsed
1	(16 oz) can Great Northern beans, drained, rinsed
1	(16 oz) can diced tomatoes
1	(16 oz) can tomato sauce
1	green pepper, chopped
1	large onion, chopped
1	(4 oz) can chopped green chilies
3	minced garlic cloves
2	tablespoon chili powder, to taste
1	tablespoon cumin seeds, to taste
1	teaspoon basil
1	teaspoon oregano
	few dashes hot sauce (optional)
	pinch of crushed red pepper (optional)

Put all ingredients except spices into a 5 quart saucepan and bring to a boil. Add spices, stir, cover partially and simmer 40 minutes. This will make a very tasty low fat dish, we like it served with tortilla chips or Golden Corn Muffins.

Serves 8-10

VARIATION: If you want a chili con carne then add one pound of cooked ground beef, drained and rinsed or one pound of cooked cubed beef to add some variety to the dish.

Golden Corn Muffins

1	cup corn meal, yellow
1	cup flour, unbleached
¼	cup honey
4	teaspoons baking powder
½	teaspoon salt
2	eggs
¾	cup buttermilk or plain yogurt
¼	cup shortening

Sift together corn meal, flour, honey, baking powder, and salt. Add eggs, milk, and shortening. Beat with a rotary beater for about 1 minute or until smooth (do not overbeat). Grease muffin tins. Fill muffin tins ⅔ full. Bake in preheated oven, 425° for 15 to 20 minutes.

Makes 12 muffins

VARIATION: One of our favorite methods for making cornbread is to bake it in a cast iron skillet, southern style. To do this take a 12 inch cast iron skillet and place 2-3 tablespoons of butter in the bottom and place into pre-heated oven. When the butter is melted remove skillet from oven and pour the corn muffin recipe into the pan and bake as usual. When cooking is done either serve directly from the skillet or turn upside down onto a plate. Cut and serve. This gives you a buttery crispy outside to an already good cornbread.

NOTE: When I was 14 this recipe won me first place in my local 4-H contest. It really is a winner.

Christmas Tree Cookie Puzzles

½   cup sugar
1   teaspoon vanilla
½   cup margarine or butter, softened
1   (3 oz) pkg. cream cheese, softened
2   cups unbleached flour

1   egg white
¼   teaspoon salt

ICING
2   cups powdered sugar
4-5   tablespoon milk
½   teaspoon mint extract (optional)
    Decorator candies, as desired

green food coloring

Preheat oven to 350° F. In large bowl, combine sugar, margarine and cream cheese; beat well. Add vanilla and egg white; blend well. Lightly spoon flour into measuring cup; level off. Stir in flour and salt mix well. Knead 1 - 2 minutes.

Divide dough into thirds. On waxed paper; press or roll each part into shape of Christmas tree, ⅛ inch thick; carefully transfer to ungreased cookie sheets.

Bake at 350° for 9 to 15 minutes or until set. Immediately cut trees into several pieces of varying shapes and sizes. Bake an additional 5 minutes; remove from cookie sheet. Cool completely.

In medium bowl, combine all icing ingredients except candies, adding enough milk until mixture is of thin spreading consistency; stir until well blended. Frost cooled tree pieces. As you frost the tree pieces place together loosely in tree shape (do not let edges touch, give them a little room to dry), then decorate tree with assorted candies. Allow icing to dry overnight if possible. Then package each cookie puzzle separately. Makes 3 tree cookie puzzles or approximately 18 servings.

VARIATION: If you want this to be a quick project, instead of icing the cookie pieces sprinkle the cookie with green colored sugar before baking. When cookie is cooled dot the cookie with little puddles of frosting and allow the children to put small candies on each dot of icing to resemble decorations on the tree.

The Fourth Wise Man

Robert O. Day

Shalom! Peace be unto you. Let me introduce myself, although my name does not matter and you could not pronounce it anyway. I am the fourth wise man. You say there were but three spoken of, true, but never-the-less I am the fourth that traveled to see where the star of Bethlehem led. Unlike the others, I did not go home, but remained near by to see what might be learned.

May I share a few things I wrote here upon this scroll, such as the beauty of the love that existed in the little Lord's family. Though born in a stable, our Lord was treated as a king. Even before He was born His mother and father spoke lovingly of Him and what he would become and do in His life. The angel had told them many things they had to ponder as they prepared to raise the Savior of the World. Such plans .... but I must not digress.

We know from the Holy Books the circumstances of the Savior's birth in the stable, the visit of the other three wise men, the wicked king Herod's action to have all children under two murdered to protect his throne and the escape of the Messiah's family into Egypt.

Isn't it wonderful that God used Jesus' family to help him in his time of need rather than sending angels to defend him. But then, that is true of all families. God always tries to work through mothers and fathers in the preparation of His little ones for the tasks they must face in the world. Mary and Joseph were warned of an angel what Jesus' tasks would be on a regular basis right through his life they seemed to use every task and teach every lesson to help the young Lord understand, develop and grow to achieve his life's mission. As it is today, they put all of their efforts into his preparation and the preparation of the Lord's brothers and sisters.

Not much is found in the Bible regarding the early life of Jesus, but he grew up and did the things most good boys of that time did. He played in the fields, worked side by side with his parents and family, watched and listened to the birds, enjoyed a cool drink of water from the stream or the well. Watched the rain fall, and went to church to be educated by the rabbis. Item by item He learned the ways of life, both mortal and spiritual until He was a man. In all things He was taught the laws of God and man and obeyed them both as instructed by his family and loved ones.

There is much more written here that could be shared, but I come this

night mainly to share with you the great lesson of the influence of families in the lives of God's children. Parents can and do have such a great influence on the preparation for the futures of their children. Children should understand and reflect that loving direction so that they can reach their full potential in life for which they have been carefully prepared.

Families are the greatest of God's creations and the ones He has always taken the greatest pride and concern over from the beginning of time. The man is not without the woman nor the woman without the man in the Lord. And they two are not complete without those things that make them a happy family.

At this time each year we share our love and joy with one another in remembrance of the Christ Child. We rejoice also in the family that helped to prepare Him for a task no other could do to bless the lives of all mankind. May I wish you the happiest of holidays and a blessing on each family.

Scented Bath Salts
Art Project/Gift Idea

MATERIALS LIST:

> *decorative bottle or decorate your own*
> *Epsom Salts*
> *scented oils**
> *food coloring (optional)*
> *plastic bag*
> *silk or dried flower nosegay*

INSTRUCTIONS:

1. In a plastic bag pour one cup of Epsom salts, 4-6 drops of scented oil and 2 or more drops of food coloring depending on intensity of color desired.

2. Twist bag closed and shake well to mix.

3. Pour bath salts into decorative bottle and close lid.

4. Make a tag with directions for your bath salts (To use in your tub: pour a third of cup of bath salts under running water. Immerse your body in warm relaxing scented bath and enjoy). Punch a hole in corner and tie around neck of bottle with cord, ribbon or floral nosegay.

VARIATIONS: You can make several different colors of bath salts using the same scent and layer them into a clear jar for a fanciful effect. You can also rubber stamp an image on the front of a muslin bag and place bath salts in bag for a single bath experience.

*Scented Oils can be purchased from a variety of places like health food stores, craft stores (look either in candle making area or cake and candy supplies). Remember it must be an oil to keep the scent from evaporating.

Cinnamon Apple Rings

15 tart medium apples (allow 1½ pounds of apples for each pint)
6   cups of sugar
3   cups water
1   (9 oz) package red cinnamon or red hot candies
4   drops red food color
36 Maraschino cherries (optional)

Wash the apples in cold water. Core and slice peeled apples into 1/4 inch rings. To prevent discoloration, drop into salt-vinegar water or ascorbic acid water.

Combine sugar, water, cinnamon candies and food color. Bring to a boil and boil four minutes. Remove from range, add drained apple rings, and allow to stand 10 minutes. This helps firm the apples.

Return to range and bring to a rolling boil, then simmer 30 minutes until apples are transparent.

Pack apples loosely into hot jars. Add six Maraschino cherries in center of apples as the jar is being filled. Bring syrup to a boil again and pour into jars, leaving 1/2-inch head space. Remove air bubbles and adjust lids.

Process in boiling water bath canner 15 minutes for pints and 20 minutes for quarts. Makes 6 pints. (Option: Instead of placing in canning jars, let cool and place in refrigerator if it is for immediate use)

Note: When I was growing up the only time I ever remember getting Cinnamon Apple Rings was at Christmas. My mother always purchased a couple of jars just for the holiday. I know if my brothers had let me I would have eaten the whole jar by myself. This recipe is just as good as the ones you buy in the store.

THE STAR

Florence M. Kingsley

Once upon a time in a country far away from here, there lived a little girl named Ruth. Ruth's home was not at all like our houses, for she lived in a little tower on top of the great stonewall that surrounded the town of Bethlehem. Ruth's father was the hotelkeeper—the Bible says the "inn keeper." This inn was not at all like our hotels, either. There was a great open yard, which was called the courtyard. All about this yard were little rooms and each traveler who came to the hotel rented one. The inn stood near the great stonewall of the city, so that as Ruth stood, one night, looking out of the tower window, she looked directly into the courtyard. It was truly a strange sight that met her eyes. So many people were coming to the inn, for the King had made a law that every man should come back to the city where his father used to live to be counted and to pay his taxes. Some of the people came on the backs of camels, with great rolls of bedding and their dishes for cooking upon the back of the beast. Some of them came on little donkeys, and on their backs too were the bedding and the dishes. Some of the people came walking—slowly; they were so tired. Many miles some of them had come. As Ruth looked down into the courtyard, she saw the camels being led to their places by their masters, she heard the snap of the whips, she saw the sparks shoot up from the fires that were kindled in the courtyard, where each person was preparing his own supper; she heard the cries of the tired, hungry little children.

Presently her mother, who was cooking supper, came over to the window and said, "Ruthie, thou shalt hide in the house until all those people are gone. Dost thou understand?"

"Yes, my mother," said the child, and she left the window to follow her mother back to the stove, limping painfully, for little Ruth was a cripple. Her mother stooped suddenly and caught the child in her arms.

"My poor little lamb. It was a mule's kick, just six years ago, that hurt your poor back and made you lame."

"Never mind, my mother. My back does not ache today, and lately when the light of the strange new star has shone down upon my bed my back has felt so much stronger and I have felt so happy, as though I could climb upon the rays of the star and up, up into the sky and above the stars!"

Her mother shook her head sadly. "Thou art not likely to climb much, now or ever, but come, the supper is ready; let us go to find your father. I wonder what keeps him."

They found the father standing at the gate of the courtyard, talking to a man and woman who had just arrived. The man was tall, with a long beard, and he led by a rope a snow white mule, on which sat the drooping figure of the woman. As Ruth and her mother came near, they heard the father say, "But I tell thee that there is no more room in the inn. Hast thou no friends where thou canst go to spend the night?" The man shook his head. "No, none," he answered. "I care not for myself, but my poor wife." Little Ruth pulled at her mother's dress. "Mother, the oxen sleep out under the stars these warm nights and the straw in the caves is clean and warm; I have made a bed there for my little lamb."

Ruth's mother bowed before the tall man. "Thou didst hear the child. It is as she says—the straw is clean and warm." The tall man bowed his head. "We shall be very glad to stay," and he helped the sweet-faced woman down from the donkey's back and led her away to the cave stable, while the little Ruth and her mother hurried up the stairs that they might send a bowl of porridge to the sweet-faced woman, and a sup of new milk, as well.

That night when little Ruth lay down in her bed, the rays of the beautiful new star shone through the window more brightly than before. They seemed to soothe the tired aching shoulders. She fell asleep and dreamed that the beautiful, bright star burst and out of it came countless angels, who sang in the night:

"Glory to God in the highest, peace on earth, good will to men." And then it was morning and her mother was bending over her and saying, "Awake, awake, little Ruth. Mother has something to tell thee." Then as the eyes opened slowly—"The angels came in the night, little one, and left a Baby to lay beside your little white lamb in the manger."

That afternoon, Ruth went with her mother to the fountain. The mother turned aside to talk to the other women of the town about the strange things heard and seen the night before, but Ruth went on and sat down by the edge of the fountain. The child, was not frightened, for strangers came often to the well, but never had she seen men who looked like the three who now came towards her. The first one, a tall man with a long white beard, came close to Ruth and said, "Canst tell us, child, where is born he that is called the King of the Jews?"

"I know of no king," she answered, "but last night while the star was shining, the angels brought a baby to lie beside my white lamb in the manger." The stranger bowed his head. "That must be he. Wilt thou show us the way to Him, my child?" So Ruth ran and her mother led the three men to the cave and "when they saw the Child, they rejoiced with exceeding great joy, and opening their gifts, they presented unto Him gold, and frankincense and myrrh," with wonderful jewels, so that Ruth's mother's eyes shone with wonder, but little Ruth saw only the Baby, which lay asleep on its mother's breast.

"If only I might hold Him in my arms," she thought, but was afraid to ask.

After a few days, the strangers left Bethlehem, all but the three—the man, whose name was Joseph, and Mary, his wife, and the Baby. Then, as of old, little Ruth played about the courtyard and the white lamb frolicked at her side. Often she dropped to her knees to press the little woolly white head against her breast, while she murmured: "My little lamb, my very, very own. I love you, lambie," and then together they would steal over to the entrance of the cave to peep in at the Baby, and always she thought, "If I only might touch his hand," but was afraid to ask. One night as she lay in her bed, she thought to herself: "Oh, I wish I had a beautiful gift for him, such as the wise men brought, but I have nothing at all to offer and I love him so much." Just then the light of the star, which was nightly fading, fell across the foot of the bed and shone full upon the white lamb which lay asleep at her feet—and then she thought of something. The next morning she arose with her face shining with joy. She dressed carefully and with the white lamb held close to her breast, went slowly and painfully down the stairway and over to the door of the cave. "I have come," she said, "to worship Him, and I have brought Him—my white lamb." The mother smiled at the lame child, then she lifted the Baby from her breast and placed Him in the arms of the little maid who knelt at her feet.

A few days after, an angel came to the father, Joseph, and told him to take the Baby and hurry to the land of Egypt, for the wicked King wanted to do it harm, and so these three—the father, mother and Baby—went by night to the far country of Egypt. And the star grew dimmer and dimmer and passed away forever from the skies over Bethlehem, but little Ruth grew straight and strong and beautiful as the almond trees in the orchard, and all the people who saw her were amazed, for Ruth was once a cripple.

"It was the light of the strange star," her mother said, but little Ruth knew it was the touch of the blessed Christ-Child, who was once folded against her heart.

Holiday Banner
Decoration

Materials List:

4 - 8 inch square blocks of muslin or white cotton fabric
assorted scraps of fabric for individual designs
Heavyweight appliqué film (like Heat & Bond®)
3 strips 1½ inches wide by 44-45 inches for interior border
3 strips 3½ inches wide by 44-45 inches for outside border
Fabric 14 x 45 inches for backing same as outside border
thin fleece
sharp scissors

Instructions:

1. Trace each of the parts of the selected appliqué design individually onto the paper side of the appliqué film. Since you can see through the film, you can lay it directly over the design in the book and trace it. Label each of the pieces.

2. Using sharp paper scissors, cut loosely around the traced designs on the appliqué film (at this point do not cut directly on the traced lines).

3. Before you fuse, check the manufacturer's instructions for the proper iron setting to use with the particular brand of appliqué film.

4. Look through your scraps of fabric and decide which pieces you will use for each part of the pattern. Note that if the fabric is very transparent you might want to make trace and additional piece and do it in white and layer it so you cannot see thru it. Fuse each piece of appliqué film with the paper side up and the webbing side against your fabric.

5. When all the pieces are fused, cut out the appliqué shapes following the tracing lines.

6. Remove the paper backing from the appliqué film. A thin fusing (glue) film will remain on the wrong side of the fabric.

7. Cut out four 8 inch squares of muslin or white cotton for the background.

8. Arrange and center all the pieces of appliqué design on the background fabric. Note that there is one picture on each block. Remember to leave a 1/4 inch border for seam allowances on the edges of the background fabric. Refer to the patterns as you position the pieces as they will indicate how all the pieces should be laid out. When everything is arranged to your liking, fuse the pieces in position with your iron. After the fabric is fused to the background you can decide whether you want to leave it as is or chose the appliqué technique you prefer: machine appliqué or buttonhole embroidery.

9. To assemble banner first cut 3 strips of fabric 1 1/2 inches wide by length of fabric.

10. Take one strip and cut 3 pieces 8 inches long. Sew 1 strip to the bottom of first block and press. Now sew second block to bottom of strip and press. Add a strip to bottom of second block and press. Sew third block to bottom of previous strip and press. Stitch third strip to bottom of third block and press. Stitch fourth block to bottom of third strip and press.

11. Sew one of long strips to one side of unit and press and trim even with bottom. Repeat on the other side.

12. Finish the process by sewing shorter strip across the top, press and trim even with side . Repeat process on the bottom of unit.

13. To make outside border, cut 3 strips 3 1/2 inches wide by length of fabric.

14. Sew one strip to each side of unit, press and trim. Sewing final strip to top, press and trim. Repeat process on bottom.

15. The Final process is to make a fabric sandwich. You do this by layering the back, the batting and the pieced top together in a sandwich type fashion. We are going to use the self-binding method. Cut your backing piece and batting the same size as your finished front appliqué

unit. Place fabric right sides together and lay on top of batting piece. Smooth the fabric out, no wrinkles. Now using straight pins, pin the seams securely so that they do not move (don't skimp on pins), even place pins within the body of the project for easier stitching. Sew 1/4 inch seam around all edges leaving a 5-6 inch opening to turn. Turn project right side out and press flat. Whipstitch opening closed.

16. We are now ready to quilt our project. How much you quilt it will be up to you. Here is the most basic machine method, but you can use the method you are most comfortable with. Smooth fabric and begin pinning through all layers radiating out from center. Use lots of pins so that you don't get puckers or fabric slides.

17. Set your machine for normal straight stitching. Choose a longer stitch length 10-12 stitches to inch, and if you have a walking foot use it otherwise release the pressure on the foot a little to make it easier to sew through the three layers. Starting in the center of the banner you are going to stitch in the ditch (that is stitch as close to the seam line as possible) to outline the block designs and borders.

18. Next stitch 1/16 inch away from the edge of the designs in each block. They call this traditional quilt stitching. Do this for all four blocks. You are now done with the basic quilting on your banner, but you can do a lot more if you want to.

19 Finally you will need to create a way to hang up your banner. One of the easiest ways is to create a sleeve or "tube" of fabric that will run the entire width of your banner. Cut a strip of fabric approximately 5 inches wide by the width of the banner. With right sides together, fold the strip in half lengthwise and sew the length of the strip. Turn the sleeve right side out and press. Hand stitch the sleeve to the back of your quilt at the top and run a wooden dowel through it.

20. Don't forget to put a label on the back of the quilt. This will make it easier for family historians to identify who made this great banner. Put whatever important information you want on it. With handwriting your label, use an extra-fine, permanent felt-tip pen to do your marking. Then fuse the label on to the back using the above appliqué method.

Angel Pattern:
This pattern can be enlarged by 10% if desired.
Select a green fabric for tree. Tree sits on hands.
Wings fit on back. You can use lace for wings.
Use lace or ribbon to decorate the bottom of dress

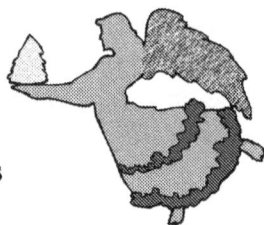

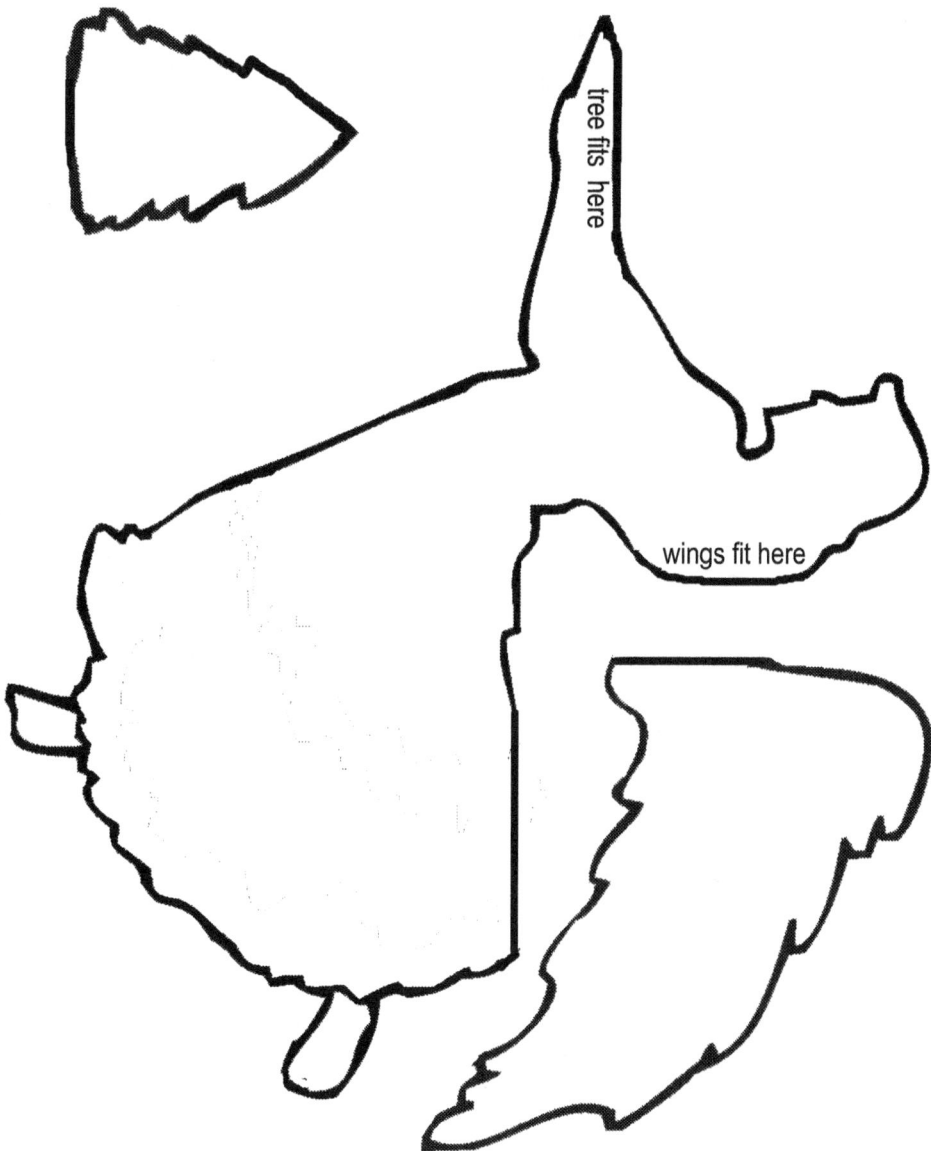

tree fits here

wings fit here

Gingerbread Man:
Select a brown fabric for gingerbread.
Glue on googly eyes or you can use buttons.
Sew buttons on body.
Paint or draw on a big smile.

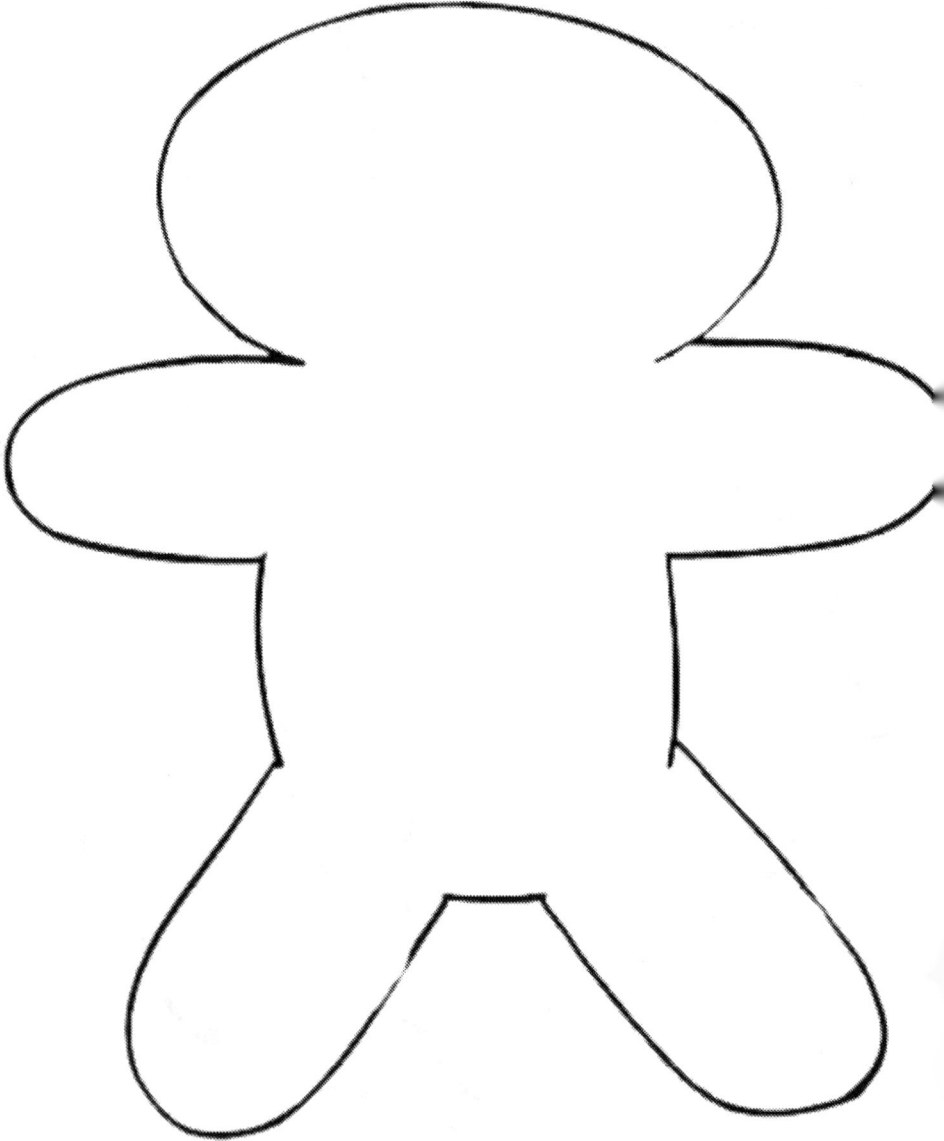

Silly Christmas Tree:

Pick a green calico or solid green fabric for tree.
Select a fun fabric for pot.
Select a brown fabric for the tree trunk.
Select a gold fabric for star or a button.
Finally decorate your tree with assorted trim or paint on
the silly face provided and paint white along edges for snow.

Candy Cane:
Select a red and white striped fabric and cut on the bias or cut candy cane
out of white and then cut red stripes to attach.
Cut out several holly leaves out of green. and a few red berries.
Finish by sewing on a piece of ribbon that can be tied into a bow.

Grandmother's Cookies

"A good Old Fashioned Cake Cookie"

1	cup shortening	2½	cups brown sugar
1	cup white sugar	3	eggs
1½	cups buttermilk	6	cups all purpose flour
3	teaspoons baking soda	2	teaspoons baking powder
1	teaspoon nutmeg	¼	teaspoon cloves
2	teaspoons cinnamon	2	teaspoon allspice
2	teaspoon vanilla	1-2	cups chopped nuts
2	12 oz package chocolate chips (optional see variations below)		

Preheat oven to 400°F. Cream shortening and sugars together in a large bowl. Add eggs. Combine dry ingredients and add alternately with buttermilk. Add vanilla, nuts and chocolate chips. The consistency of the dough will resemble a thick cake batter. Drop by spoon onto a greased cookie sheet. Bake at 400° F. for 10-12 minutes or until set.

Makes 12-15 dozen cookies

NOTE & VARIATIONS: As a child we made these cookies every year at Christmas and as they came out of the oven we would count how many cookies we had made on the steamy kitchen windows. Because it made so many cookies we used to divide the batter into four different bowls and add different ingredients. In one bowl we would add a bag of chocolate chips, in bowl two a mashed banana, in bowl three ½ cup peanut butter, and in bowl four a cup of oatmeal and raisins. Sometimes we would shake on multi-colored sprinkles or sugars. There are many things you might add to this very tasty and fragrant cake cookie. For instance diced candied fruit, butterscotch chips, mint chocolate chips, sunflower seeds, mini M&M's, etc. ... .

The Tale of the Nutcracker*

Based on the Ballet by Peter Tchaikovsky

On Christmas, Marie and her brothers had a fine big Christmas tree. It shone with lighted candles. Its branches were draped with strings of popcorn and hung with honey-cakes, sugar-plums, oranges, cookies, candy, dolls, tin soldiers and many other toys. The children's mother and father, with a crowd of merry guests, all gathered around the tree to give the presents out. But, while they were doing this, jolly Uncle Thomas came in quite loaded down with gifts. To each of the children he gave a doll that could walk and talk; but to Marie, he handed another wonderful gift, the one she like best of all. It was a wooden nutcracker having the head of a man who cracked nuts between his jaws.

How Marie loved that nutcracker! She carried it around in her arms till her little brother Fritz, snatched it from her and broke it. Marie burst into tears. She picked up the broken nutcracker, and soothed him in her arms. Then she put him in a little doll's cradle and gently rocked him to sleep.

When the Christmas party was over, the candles were all put out and the family went up to bed. But Marie could not go to sleep for thinking of her nutcracker. At last she got up quietly and stole down the stairs to see him. But what did she see now? The Christmas tree grew up tall before her eyes. Again it was all a great blaze of light. The dolls and other toys came down from the branches where thy hung and started in to dance. And Marie heard music, gay lively music, with the piping of shrill little flues and the silver chiming of bells.

The toys were all dancing merrily to that music when suddenly there came scampering into the room an army of little mice. They had come to eat up the sweets that still hung on the tree. So the toys lined up in a hurry. Led by the Nutcracker, they started to fight the army of mice. What a battle they fought! It was a terrific tussle. At last, King Mouse, the leader of the band of tiny robbers, fought hand to hand with Nutcracker. Then little Marie, afraid that her beloved Nutcracker might get hurt in the fray, threw her shoe at King Mouse. Instantly the mice scattered, running in all directions and scampering off to their holes.

But now that the battle was over, a very strange thing happened. Nutcracker all at once changed into a man, a fine young prince. Politely he bowed and kissed the hand of little Marie, and he asked her to fly with

62

him far away to a beautiful place full of goodies, a place that was called Jam Mountain. Jam Mountain! Oh, Jam Mountain! What little girl would not like to fly to such a place? Marie said yes at once and off they went on their way. The flew over forests and plains in company with the fluffy little white snowflake fairies and soon they reached Jam Mountain.

What a land that was! It had a mountain of strawberry jam with piles of sugar on top. All kinds of candy came running to meet them and along with the candy, a lovely little lady, the Sugar-Plum Fairy, came flying on shining wings. Gaily she greeted the Prince and Marie. Then a great feast was held in their honor. The green and yellow stick candies and the pink and white striped stick candies and the chocolates, and other goodies all began to dance. Even brown coffee-berries from Java, and dignified tea leaves from China, joined in the merrymaking.

Flowers danced a gay little waltz. The toy pipes danced a polka and the Sugar-Plum Fairy herself went lightly tripping and twirling, skipping and twinkling and sparkling, nodding her head and bowing most prettily to Marie. Again there was sprightly music, lively, brisk, and gay.

But, just at that moment, Marie suddenly opened her eyes. In the moonlight she saw the snow lying white on neighboring rooftops, the bare black branches of trees, laden down with the snow and little soft drifts of snowflakes piled high on her window sill. Where was she? What a surprise! She was not in the land of the little Sugar-Plum Fairy. She was lying on her own little bed upstairs in her own little room and she had only been dreaming! And Nutcracker? What of Nutcracker? He was in his cradle where she would find him in the morning.

Peter Tchaikovsky wrote the music of his Nutcracker Suite as a ballet for Russian children to dance to. If you listen to the music it sounds as if the toys are actually marching around the Christmas tree.

Holiday Cone Boxes
Art Project/Decoration/Gift Idea

MATERIALS LIST:

> *old Christmas cards or index weight paper*
> *scissors*
> *pencil*
> *ruler*
> *bread knife*
> *glue*
> *cord for loops*

INSTRUCTIONS:

1. Trace cone pattern. Open up Christmas card and lay on table picture side down. Transfer cone pattern to back of picture side of card.

2. Cut around outline of box.

3. Line up your ruler on each line and use a butter knife to score each line (that means press down hard on the line to make an impression). Crease along the scored lines bending cone into shape.

4. Spread glue along the side flap and press to stick. Pierce a hole through the center of the lid. Re-crease along the fold lines to shape the box.

5. Spread glue along the side flap and press to stick, this will form the cone. If you are in a hurry try double-stik tape.

6. Thread a loop of cord through the hole in the lid and knot on the underside.

7. To fasten the lid closed, stick a little double-sided tape on the right side of the lid flaps. Place flaps inside the box and press to seal.

VARIATION: Using old Christmas cards is a great way to recycle, but if your a little short on Christmas cards try using index weight paper and glue on bright cheery wrapping paper to the outside, paint your own design on it or cover it with fabric. Then add decorative splashes with bits of lace, ribbons and glitter.

SUGGESTIONS: Tired of advent calendars, make and number twenty-four cone boxes and fill them with special treats and hang them on the tree. Allow the children to take off one cone each day till Christmas. Lots more fun than opening windows on an oversized card.

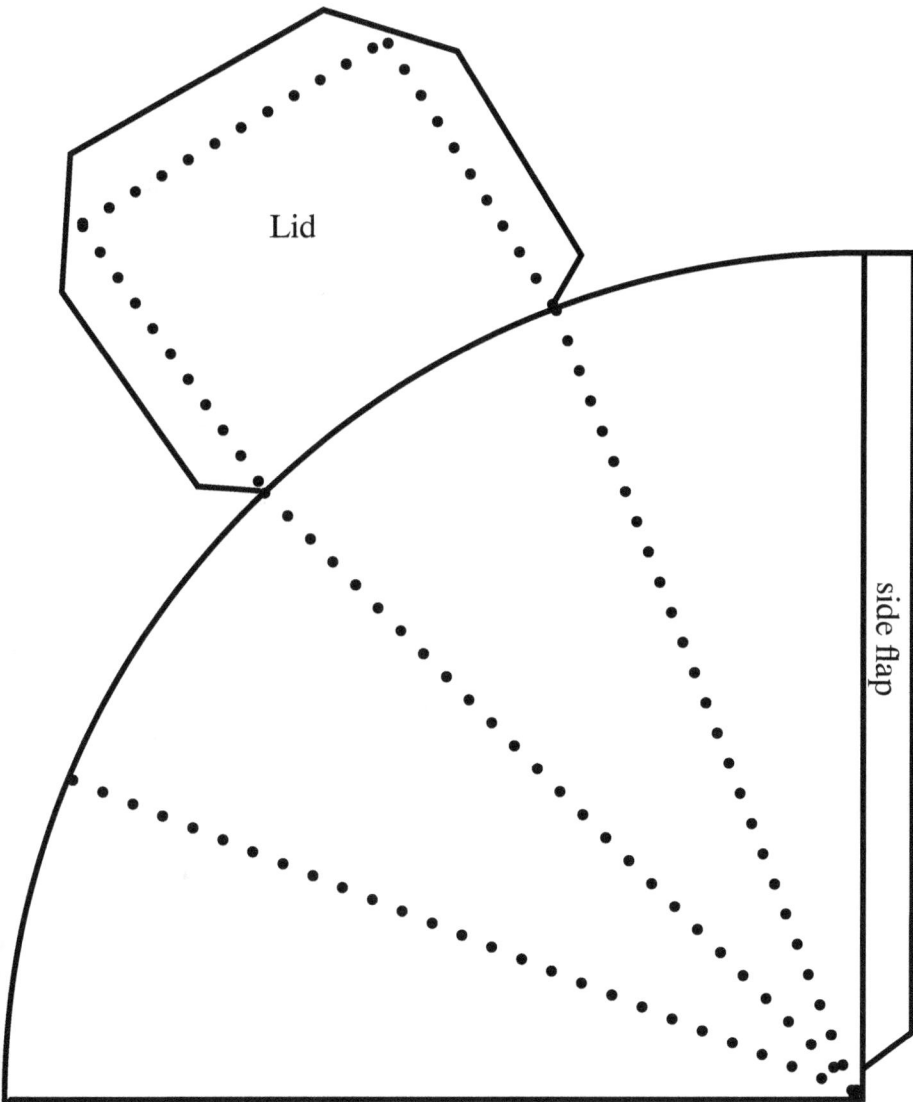

Lid

side flap

Cinnamon Crunch Nuts

These Nuts are Heavenly - Food of the Gods"
Rick Potter - Food Taster

1	cup almonds
1	cup pecans
1	cup walnuts
2	tablespoon butter or margarine
½	cup light corn syrup
¼	cup sugar
2	tablespoon cinnamon
¼	cup sugar

Place nuts on a 9x13 pan. Heat in oven at 250° for 5 minutes. In a sauce-pan, melt butter over medium heat. Stir in corn syrup, ¼ cup sugar and cinnamon. Bring to a boil, stirring constantly in a figure 8 configuration. After it arrives at the boil, let it boil for 5 minutes without stirring.

Pour hot syrup over nuts, stirring nuts constantly to coat evenly. Bake in oven at 250° for 1 hour, stirring several times. Remove from oven and sprinkle remaining ¼ cup sugar over nuts. Immediately spread nuts onto greased sheets and separate into individual nuts. Store in tightly covered containers.

Makes 3 cups of nuts

Gift Suggestion After the nuts have cooled. Place into decorated paper cones (see previous page) and hang on your Christmas tree, give as gifts, or use as party favors.

"

An Adventure Stick for Christmas

Robert O. Day

My name's Casey, I'm six years old, and I was named for my grandfather Casey O'Toole. Yes, I have red hair and freckles, but that wasn't my idea, neither was the green eyes I have to look out of every day. My Momma and Dad say there's nothing about me that's not special, but after what I got in my Christmas sock this year I'm not so sure.

Ya' see, we're poor, I mean, we don't have much money. And what money my Dad does make we use up just payin' for things like food and rent and doctor bills. I never git' an allowance, like the other kids talk about at school, I don't wear fancy clothes or have a bunch of fancy toys un' stuff. And nobody can help it, that's just the way things are. Which is why Christmas at my house is different.

Every year my Dad and I go out into the woods at the end of town and chop us down a little tree. We take it home and nail some wood onto it for a base and sit it in the corner of the front room. It's always a little tree, cuz' we don't have much room, but that's O.K., cuz' we don't have much to put under it anyway.

We always decorate the tree with all of the "pretties" that God leaves for the poor like us to find. Things like holly berries, little pine cones, pea pods, anything that can be strung on a thread or string to hang on the tree. And every year at school when we can make things for Christmas, my sister Shawna and I always make paper snow flakes and a star for the top of the tree. Sometimes other kids don't want to take the things they make home, so we take them home for our tree. When we're finished, it's always a beauty, and even without electric lights and strings of tinsel, the tree sparkles. And it smells like the forest, all piney and clean.

Oh, yes, there is always one other thing we do every year after Momma puts up the Nativity scene on the fireplace mantle, Shawna and me hang up a sock, and hope that some little goody is left inside. It's never very much, but it's always a surprise. One year we each got a peanut, another year a stick of chewing gum. But this year it was the biggest surprise of all. Shawna got a spool of thread with a needle stuck in it and I got a STICK.

That's what I said, a stick, about two feet long, kinda' knobby...you

know...bigger and rounder that the rest of the stick. It didn't have any bark on it and was smooth like someone had spent allot of time polishing it. When I saw it stickin' outa' my sock I thought there must be something on the other end, but after I took it out, the other end looked just like the part that was sticking out.

I was so surprised at just getting a stick for Christmas, I just sat right down cross legged on the floor and stared at it. What in the world would I ever do with that, it must be a mistake or a joke, nobody gets a stick for a Christmas present! I hit the floor with it; I smelled it; I held it up against the light to see if anything was written on it; I stuck my tongue on it to see if maybe it was good to eat, but it was just a plain old stick.

Just about the time I started hitting myself on the head with it, Dad and Grandpa O'Toole came through the door. Grandpa slapped my Dad on the back, and while grinning from ear to ear, said: "So you gave it to him already!"

"Sure!" Dad said, "I didn't want him to have to wait to enjoy the best gift we have ever been able to give him for Christmas, so I left it in his Christmas sock."

"Lucky boy!" said Grandpa, "I never gave you your Adventure Stick until you were 10; it was for your birthday."

Grandpa and Dad hurried across the room and bent over me smiling and giggling so much, I thought it must be a joke for sure. So I asked them, "What's the trick? What's an Adventure Stick?"

"You mean," said Grandpa, standing up and looking down at Dad, "that he doesn't know what an Adventure Stick is? You've never told him? You never told him about the one you had?" Dad sadly shook his head no, and grandpa threw his hands up in the air and sighed, "I just can't believe that. I can't, I can't, I can't."

"Sorry," said Dad, "I'll tell him right now."

But Grandpa was sitting down in the rocking chair, that's what he always does when he has something to say that he thinks is really important. "Nope! You had your chance. I'll explain it to him. After all, he'll have to understand just how important it is to fully use his imagination if he is going to get the most from his Adventure Stick. He needs to know that they are not given to just anyone. Come over here and sit down in front of me Casey, and I'll explain what a wonderful gift you've received."

That sounded a whole lot like a long "you need to do it my way" invitation to me, and I looked first at the stick in my hand, and then at my Dad. I asked him with my eyes if this was all really necessary?, and Dad

nodded his head and smiled. So I slowly walked across the room, with my head down, and flopped on the floor, cross-legged, in front of Grandpa and stared at my feet. I just know this is going to last a long time, an' I can smell Momma fixin' oatmeal with raisins. I'm just going to starve to death!

Dad must have understood that I wasn't happy about things, because he came up behind me and messed up my hair, the way he always does when he want's to let me know everything's all right. I jerked my head to one side to let him know it wasn't workin', but just the same I was glad he was there, cuz he knew how Grandpa could talk and talk and talk about things. You know, I'll bet he had the same thing happen to him when he was a kid!

"Now Casey," Grandpa began, "an adventure stick is a very wondrous and special thing. It's not for everybody, but only for special people, with special qualities. Do you understand?"

"Yes Grandpa," I muttered, still looking down at my foot, "but what makes **me** so special?"

"What makes you?...are you serious?...Why your great-great-great-great-great grandfather many years ago in Ireland made it special for all of us O'Tooles, when he caught the King of the Little People! Gracious me, I thought everyone in the family knew that story!"

"I heard of it Grandpa, but I don't know what a little people is, and what's so important about catching the king of the little people? Especially that long ago, that must have been back when there were dinosaurs." I muttered.

"Dinosaurs indeed! Anyone can see their bones in a museum, but only a very special few have ever seen the little people of the Emerald Isle."

Looking up I asked, "What's an Emerald Isle?"

"Don't tell me you don't know what the Emerald Isle is, Oh the Saints preserve us!" Grandpa gasped and took off his hat and held it over his heart. "That's our ancient home land Casey, that's Ireland, that's where our family goes back two dozen generations. And before that they must have come from heaven."

With that one I had to scratch my head real hard, "Huh? Grandpa, what do you mean?"

"Never mind," Grandpa said as he put his hat back on his head and leaned back into the chair. "We'll save the geography and genealogy until some other time."

"Huh?"

Dad had now kneeled down, put his arm around me and gave me a squeeze. "Don't worry Casey my boy, right now we're just going to talk about your special Christmas present. Right Grandpa?"

"Right! By all means, although I will have to explain the little kings promise. You see, if you catch one of the little people, they have to give you a gift so you will let them go. The gift that was given to the O'Toole's was that the oldest male child in the family forever and ever would be blessed with an Adventure Stick when he was old enough to appreciate it. And you were given your stick for Christmas because we think you are now old enough." Having said that Grandpa leaned forward, lifted my chin up with his hand, and looked me straight in the eye. "You are old enough aren't you?"

"Of course, I mean I guess, I mean...how do I know? What is an Adventure Stick anyway? What do I do with it?" And lifting it up, I turned it back and forth in the air. "It just looks like a plain ole' smooth stick to me! I guess I could hit rocks with it."

"Rocks? Oh, my stars no, that might damage the magic!" Dad sputtered and stood straight up, taking the stick out of my hand and hiding it behind him. "Maybe he's not ready for it yet, Grandpa. Maybe he'll have to wait a year or two."

Grandpa got up out of his chair, and he and my Dad walked across the room to the door where they stood with their backs to me and whispered things back and forth to each other. Finally, after what seemed to be a very long time, they turned around and walked back across the room and stood over me, wearing very serious faces.

"Casey, before we can show you how the Adventure Stick works, we have to know if you have a good imagination." Dad said.

"Yes, Casey, you have to be able to pretend, and to do a good job of it, or the magic of the Stick won't work for you and it will all be a waste." Then Grandpa just stood and looked at me for a long time. "Do you have any imagination? Can you pretend and really mean it?"

That question made me mighty mad, cuz' I'm a good pretender. I can imagine anything I want and it's as real as real could be. " Grandpa, Dad, you have to be kidding! I'm the best there ever was, ever!"

Dad smiled a little smile at me and said, "Oh yea, then let's see you prove it. Pretend to be a....a....a mouse."

And I did. I was the best mouse in the house. Then Grandpa wanted me to be a monkey. So I became a big ape that beat his chest and screamed

real loud. Then they wanted an airplane, a fish, a monster, my school teacher, and about a hundred other things. And I did them all.

Then Mom called us in for breakfast. We sat down at the table, had a blessing on the food, and then Dad did the strangest thing. He handed me the Adventure Stick and said, "All right, let's see if your ready to use the Stick's magic yet. Hold it in you right hand, and while waving one end of it over your bowl of oatmeal, make the stick become a magic wand and turn your oatmeal into a delicious bowl of chocolate ice cream with fudge sauce and nuts."

I took the Stick from Dad, and I wondered down deep inside if I could really do that. But I made up my mind that if there was any magic in the Adventure Stick, I had the power to pull it out because I have the best imagination in the world. So....pulling up all of my powers and drawing them into the stick, I waved my magic wand over the oatmeal and **Bam! Pam! Pow!** it became chocolate ice cream with fudge sauce and nuts.

Quickly I put down the Adventure Stick and picked up my spoon. I scooped up a big spoonful of ice cream and nuts, and stuffed it into my mouth. Oh, my but it's cold, and sweet and wonderful. And I smiled a big, big smile as it melted in my mouth, ran over my tongue and down my throat. Then I took another spoonful, and another, until it was all gone.

Everyone around the table was looking at me with their mouths open, and Momma said, "What in the world is the matter with that boy? Why is he eating his oatmeal like that. Does he really think he had turned it into ice cream?"

And my sister Shawna giggled, "Look at him, he's chewing his raisins just like they are nuts. Maybe he's the one that nuts Momma!"

"No," said Grandpa, "He's not nuts, he's really eating ice cream with nuts and things, compliments of his new Adventure Stick. He's finally learned how to use it! Isn't that just the most wondrous thing!"

"When do I get my stick, Grandpa? How come Casey got one and I didn't? Is that really fair? How come! How come!" Shawn whined.

"Only the oldest boy gets the Adventure Stick," I yelled, "It's not for girls! Right Grandpa? Right Dad?"

"I'm afraid so, Shawna," Dad said with a sigh, "It may not seem fair right now, but after breakfast we'll sit down in the living room and Grandpa can explain it to you."

"This I've got to hear, sounds like a bit of Irish blarney to me!" said Mom, and she winked at Shawna. "Maybe we girls have a thing or two

that we can tell you that you don't know as well, right Shawna?" And my sister smiled and winked back. I wonder what those two are up to?

Of course there's lots I could tell you about what else went on all Christmas Day, about who did what and when. And how many adventures I went on that day with the use of my wonderful Adventure Stick, but these are stories for some other time.

I want to tell you what happened when we went back to school after the holidays were over. The second day back was "Show and Tell Day" and everyone was supposed to bring their favorite Christmas present to show to the class. Henry brought a new 3 foot tall robot that operated by remote control. When you pushed buttons on the control box it said and did things, but always the same things, nothing different. Sally brought a talking Barbie doll, with hair so long it touched her feet, and even though it could talk, it could only say the same things over and over again.

John brought in a little wind up train that ran on a track, that went around and around and around. And you had to keep winding it up. Jim had a ray gun that sparked and buzzed when you pulled the trigger. It was real neat, until the batteries ran out, then it wouldn't do anything. Mary Ann brought her little fish bowl with 5 fish in it. At the bottom of the bowl was a castle with a hole the fish could swim through when they felt like it, which wasn't very often. It was fun watching the fish for a little while, but when they just kept doing the same thing over and over again, it got boring.

Everyone in class "Showed and Telled" their things, until at last it was my turn. Boy were they ever going to be surprised. I walked up to the front of the class and waited until everyone was looking at me, and then I pulled out my Adventure Stick and held it up by one end so everyone could get a good look. I even walked up and down each isle so that everyone could get a closer look, then I went back to the front of the room.

All the kids started to giggle and talk and point at my Stick. They wanted to know why I would bring an old stick to school?, and was that my Christmas present? Some even called me stupid and crazy. Mrs. Martin, our teacher, didn't like that and she made the class be quiet.

She told them, "You shouldn't make fun of Casey and be making such rude remarks until you find out what he has to 'Show and Tell' you." That made everyone sit down and be quiet. And they all just sat there, staring at me with big eyes. They waiting for me to say or do something that would let them make fun of me again. But I didn't care. I knew what my

Adventure Stick could do, and I felt sorry for them that they couldn't have one. They had to play with those boring old toys and things that just kept doing the same thing over and over again. My stick can make anything happen in any way I wish, all I have to do is imagine it and it happens.

I told them in a nice loud voice, "You think that this is just an old stick, but you're wrong. This is a very special **Adventure** Stick that allows me to go anywhere I wish, be anything I wish, and do anything I can imagine. It holds the greatest magic in the world, the power to create anything from nothing, just by thinking it. I have made oatmeal with raisins into ice cream with fudge sauce and nuts. I have been an astronaut and taken a trip to Mars and back. Just last night I went to the north pole and visited Santa Claus, his reindeer, his elves and saw his toy factory. And I ate gum drops and candy canes until I was so full I was about to bust. I even turned an old toad into a handsome prince and sent him on a trip in a royal coach to London town. When I go home this afternoon I think I'll create a whaling ship and sail out to sea for a while, at least until supper time. This is the greatest present in the whole world."

Everyone in class thought I was crazy and no one wanted to play with me. But they soon changed their mind when they saw how much fun I was having at recess and after school with my Adventure Stick. One by one my friends came over and asked me how it worked, and one by one I tried to explain it to them.

Finally, I invited five of them to go with me on an Indian hunting party. After school we went off to the park and found a spot under the large oak tree, where I told them to sit cross-legged Indian style on the ground. We made a circle around some rocks I placed in the open space of the circle. Then I told them, "Cross your arms, close your eyes and look deep into your imagination until you see six braves sitting around a roaring fire. In your ears you must hear the beat of tom-toms, on your face a breeze is blowing, in your nose your can smell the fire, on your feet you feel moccasins and your clothes are made of deer skins. Do you see it? Do you feel it? Do you smell it? I now wave over all our heads the Adventure Stick to make the magic. In your imagination you are taking the place of one of those Indian Braves seated around the council fire. Is it not so?

And all of the braves answered, "It is so."

"Now open your eyes and be that brave until the Adventure Stick releases you back into the real world. Look! See! Touch! Smell! You are there, my Indian brothers."

And it really was so. Six Indians sat in full Indian dress around the council fire. I as the chief spoke to the others, "The time has come my brothers for us to take the canoe and paddle up river to find the deer, that we may shoot them with our arrows and bring home food for our families. Get your paddles and follow me to the canoe and we will leave now. Will you make it so?"

And they all answered, "We will make it so." Each brave got up from the ground and went under the tree where he found a paddle. Then all walked in a straight line behind me, their chief, until we reached the river. There we sat the canoe into the water and we waded into the water, then each of us took his place. Red Fox sat beside me in the front of the canoe, behind us sat Running Dog and Small Turtle, then Soaring Eagle and Sitting Horse.

"Let us drift into the center of the river before we start to paddle," I said to my braves. When we reached the middle of the river I called out, "Now, brave hunters, together let us paddle." And we each put our paddles into the water and paddled the canoe quietly and quickly up the stream.

Suddenly a voice was heard calling, "Mom, what are those boys doing over there? Why are they sitting on the ground and waving sticks back and forth? What's going on?" Then another voice, "I don't know Sarah, and I don't care, just forget about them it's time to go home."

Ignoring everything around us, I whispered, "Quiet! Stop paddling for a moment! Did you hear that? Look, it's two deer standing there among the forest. Paddle quietly to shore and sneak through the trees so they can not see nor hear you. When everyone is ready I will give a war cry. Then let your arrows fly toward the deer that we may shoot them and take them home to feed our families."

Quietly we paddled to the shore and everyone did what I said. When all had reached their place I stood up and gave a war cry, "Whooooppooop-pooppaaahhhh!"

Everyone jumped up, shot their arrows and ran screaming toward the place where the two deer were trying to run away. But it was too late, every arrow had found its mark.

"Mom!" The little girl shrieked, "those boys are coming after us! Why are they yelling and chasing us? Help Momma! Help!" The mother grabbed the little girl up into her arms and ran out of the park as fast as she could go, yelling, "Help! Police!"

Now we reached the spot where the deer were lying on the ground full of arrows. It was too bad that they had to die, but our families needed to

eat. "Clean the deer and we will go back to camp." I said, and they did so right away. Then Sitting Horse and Running Dog put the deer around their shoulders and we all headed back to camp singing a hunting song.

At camp, we gave the deer to the women to cook and the braves danced around the fire until it was time to eat. After eating lots and lots of deer, we went to our tents to sleep for the night. And I decided it was time that we all went home, so I waved the Adventure Stick over us all and we quickly changed back into what we had been when school had ended. Then everyone went home wiser and happier. And they all told me how much they wished they had and Adventure Stick, but I told them I would take them with me anytime they wanted to.....and I did too.

Home alone, or with other people, my Adventure Stick turned out to be the best Christmas present anyone in the whole world ever received. And to think, that only the first born O'Toole boys could have one didn't seem right. So one day, using the Stick, I took a whole bunch of my friends to Ireland, where we captured the King of the Little People and made him agree to give anyone with a good enough imagination the right to have an Adventure Stick of their own. And from that day until this, that's just the way it has been.

And how about you? How's your imagination? If you're tired of having toys that do all the playing while you just watch, maybe you need to get an Adventure Stick of your own and start having some **real fun** too! It's never too late......

As for me and my Adventure Stick, we still have lots of places to go and adventures by the hundreds, but those are tales for another time..... Right?

Linda S. Day ©1997

Pinwheels
Art Activity/Decoration

MATERIALS LIST:

pencil with eraser
index weight paper
2 small beads or pearls
quilting straight pin
nail
colored markers or scraps of
  wrapping paper (glue stick)

INSTRUCTIONS:

1. Cut an 8 1/2 inch square piece of index paper. Decorate one side of paper with colored markers or crayons or cut an 8 1/2 inch piece of wrapping paper and glue to one side of the index paper.

2. Mark center of paper with a dot. Draw lines diagonally from corner to corner, stopping 1 1/4 inches from center point. Cut from the corners along each line up to mark. (see diagram 1)

3. Using a nail, push a hole in the center of square. Mark and make a hole 3/4 inch from each corner in the middle of each right-hand section.

4. Using pinking shears cut a 2 inch circle from leftover index paper. Make a hole in center of circle.

5. Thread the quilting pin through 1 bead, then through the circle, then through the hole in each section of the pinwheel in turn, bending the sails to the middle. (diagram 2) Now push the pin through the center hole in the pinwheel, through the second bead and push the pin into the eraser. Now blow and watch your pinwheel spin.

NOTE: You can make this pinwheel in a variety of sizes. To make pinwheel bows for packages follow steps 1-2 above. Instead of putting a pin through the center of each hole, simple glue each point of the pinwheel to the center (hold each corner until glue sets) and place a contrasting color circle over center (optional). For bows, a 3 or 4 inch square works best.

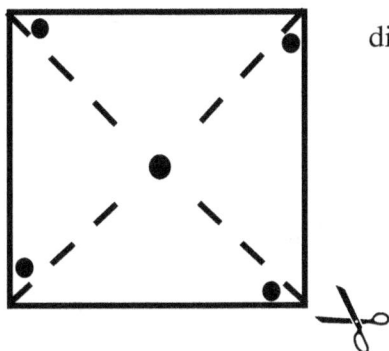

diagram 1

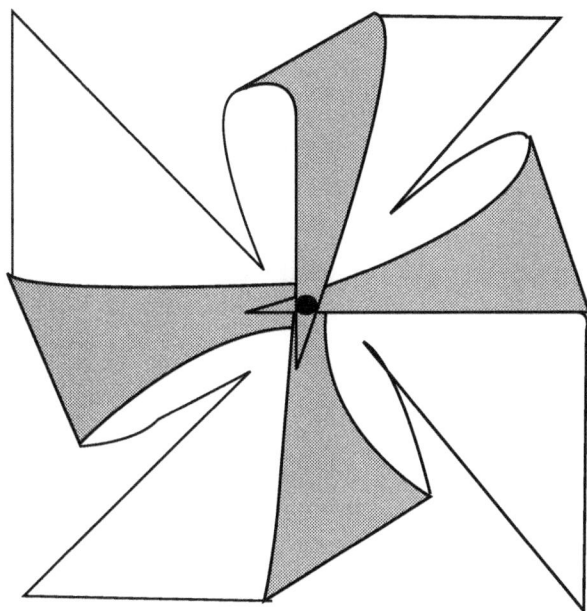

diagram 2

Crescent Christmas Tree

2   cans Crescent Dinner Rolls
2   tablespoons margarine softened
2   tablespoons sugar
1   teaspoon cinnamon

Glaze
½   cup powdered sugar
1   tablespoon milk
¼   teaspoon vanilla
     Red & Green candied cherries halved

Heat oven to 375°F. Lightly grease cookie sheet. Separate dough into 4 rectangles. Firmly press perforations to seal. Spread each rectangle with margarine. In small bowl, combine sugar, and cinnamon; sprinkle evenly over rectangles. Starting at shorter side, roll crosswise into 3 equal slices. Place slices, cut side down on greased cookie sheet to form tree. Begin with 1 slice for top; arrange 2 slices just below, with sides closely touching. Continue arranging a row of 3 slices, then a row of 4 slices. Use the remaining 2 slices for the trunk. Bake at 375°F for 15 to 20 minutes or until deep golden brown. Cool 3 minutes; carefully remove from cookie sheet. Cool slightly on wire rack.

In small bowl, combine powdered sugar, milk and vanilla until smooth; drizzle over tree. Garnish with candied cherry halves or various small candies.

Makes 12 rolls

Gift Suggestion: After removing tree from cookie sheet, place on bread board, finishing decorating per instructions. Attach ribbon to breadboard and give as a gift. Or maybe just give it on the cookie sheet as a gift, everyone can use an extra cookie sheet.

The Elves and the Shoemaker

as told by MyLinda Butterworth
based on a German folk tale

ONCE there was a shoemaker who worked hard and was very honest. Even so, he was as poor as a church mouse and could not earn enough to support himself and his wife. At last there came a time when all he had left was one piece of leather—just large enough to be made into one pair of shoes. The shoemaker cut the leather into pieces ready to stitch and make into shoes the next day. He left them on his work bench, intending to get up with the sun and start to work. The shoemaker was a good man, so his heart was light despite all his troubles. He went to bed peacefully, trusting that he would be able to finish the shoes the next day and sell them. Leaving all his cares to heaven, he settled his head on his pillow and fell asleep.

Bright and early the next morning the shoemaker rose and went to his work bench. To his amazement, there on the table were two shoes, already finished. They were beautifully made, neat and true, and with not a stitch out of place. But there was no sign that anyone had been in the house. The good man and his wife could not imagine how the shoes could have been made while they slept.

The first customer who came in the morning was so pleased with the shoes that he bought them immediately. The price he paid was enough that the shoemaker was now able to buy enough leather to make two more pairs of shoes.

The next evening the shoemaker cut out two pairs of shoes and went to bed early, as before. When he got up in the morning , there were the shoes on his bench, all finished and perfectly made just as before. Once again there was no sign that anyone had been in the house.

That day customers came in who paid the shoemaker handsomely for his goods, so he was able to buy leather for four pairs of shoes. Once again he cut out the shoes and left the pieces on the bench. Once again he found in the morning that all four pairs of shoes were made.

For some time the same thing happened, until the good man and his wife were thriving and prosperous. But they were not satisfied to have so much done for them and not know to whom they should be grateful. One evening about Christmas time, as they were sitting near the fire and chatting together, the shoemaker said to his wife, "I would like to stay up tonight so that we might see who it is who comes in during the night and makes the beautiful shoes we find each morning."

The wife agreed, so they hid themselves behind a curtain and waited to see what would happen. Just as the clock struck twelve, two tiny elves came dancing into the room. They hopped upon the bench, took up the work that was cut out, and began with their tiny little fingers to stitch, sew, and hammer so neatly and quickly that the shoemaker could not believe his eyes. These little elves wore nothing. They worked with tiny scissors and hammers and thread, and as they worked they sang this song:

We stitch and clip and hammer,
These shoes we'll make for you,
We're happy when we do good deeds,
Then we're quickly out of view!

No one ever worked so fast, as those two little elves did. They worked on until the job was quite finished and the shoes stood ready for use upon the table. Then they took hold of each other's hands and ran swiftly away, leaving the room as it was before.

"These little elves have made us rich and happy," said the shoemaker to his wife. "How can we thank them and do them a good service in return?"

"They were running around with nothing on, and must be frozen with the cold. I will make them tiny coats, pants and a cap," said the wife.

"And I will make them each a little pair of shoes," said her husband.

That very day they went about their tasks. The wife cut out two tiny pairs of yellow trousers; two teeny, weeny blue coats; and two bits of caps, bright orange, because she thought the elves would like bright colors; and her husband made two little pairs of shoes with long, pointed toes. They made the wee clothes as dainty as could be, with nice little stitches and pretty buttons, and by Christmas time they were finished.

On Christmas eve the shoemaker cleaned his bench, and on it, instead of leather, he laid the two sets of clothing and the tiny shoes. Then he and his wife hid away as before to see what the elves would do.

Promptly at midnight, they came skipping in and were about to set to work. But instead of the leather cut and ready to assemble they found the charming little clothes and shoe. At first they were surprised, then excessively delighted. In the twinkling of an eye they put on and smoothed down the pretty clothes. Then they began to dance and sing in a circle:

"Now we're boys so fine and neat,
Why cobble more for other's feet?"

When the sun rose, they danced out of the window, over the green, and out of sight. The shoemaker and his wife never saw them again, but continued to do well, and had good luck for the rest of their lives.

No Bake Graham Cracker House
Art Project/Decoration

MATERIALS LIST:

Graham crackers (plain or chocolate)	wax paper
bowl of Royal icing	knife for spreading
index card	scissors
sugar cones	small bowl
spoon	toothpicks

little candies (gumdrops, M&M's®, sprinkles, candy canes, life savers, etc.)

INSTRUCTIONS:

1. To make the walls of each house, lay one graham cracker on a sheet of waxed paper. Put icing around the edges of four other graham crackers. Stand them around the one that is on the waxed paper. Let the icing dry.

2. To make roof, fold an index card in half. Apply frosting to card. Place 3 sections of cracker on each side of fold to make roof. Place it on top of graham cracker walls.

3. From an index card, cut two triangles that are big enough to fill in the holes at either end of the roof line and house. Spread icing on the triangles and then place them over the holes.

4. Cut windows and doors from graham cracker quarters and "glue" on with icing onto the house. Decorate the house with more icing and lot of little candies.

5. Make more houses to make a village. Have fun ... be creative! Set all of the houses aside to dry.

6. Take a toothpick and place three marshmallows on it to make a snowman. Then use additional toothpicks to make arms. Use a fine line marker to make a face.

7. To make sugar cone Christmas trees, take some royal icing and place in a separate bowl. Mix green food coloring with the icing. Spread

icing on the outside of sugar cones. Shake candy sprinkles over the icing. Let the icing dry.

8. Set up your graham cracker village, snowmen and trees on a tray. Add candy walkways. Then sprinkle with white paper holes to make snow

Royal Icing

2   egg whites
3½   cups powdered sugar
2   tablespoons lemon juice
          blue food coloring, to prevent icing from turning gray

1. In a large bowl with an electric mixer, beat egg whites until stiff but not dry, 2 to 3 minutes.

2. With beaters running, gradually sift sugar into whites until well mixed. Beat in lemon juice and 1 very small drop food coloring until mixture is of spreading consistency.

Jolly Elf Fudge Nut Bars

"Yummy to eat and easy to make" Whitney Allen - Kitchen Tester

1	cup butter or margarine
2	cups light brown sugar
2	eggs, beaten
1	teaspoon vanilla
2½	cups flour
1	teaspoon salt
1	teaspoon baking soda
3	cups quick-cooking oats

Preheat oven to 350° F. Cream margarine and brown sugar; add eggs and vanilla. Sift flour, baking soda, and salt; add to creamed mixture. Mix in oatmeal and set aside while you make the filling.

FILLING:

1	12-ounce package chocolate chips
2	tablespoons butter or margarine
1	cup sweetened condensed milk
½	teaspoon salt
1	cup chopped nuts
2	teaspoon vanilla

In a heavy saucepan mix sweetened condensed milk, chocolate chips, and margarine over medium heat till melted. Stir in vanilla and nuts till smooth. Press about ⅔ of oatmeal mixture into the bottom of a greased 9 x 13 inch pan. Spread chocolate filling over oatmeal mixture. Crumble remaining ⅓ of dough over filling. Bake 25 - 30 minutes or until brown. Cool; then cut into bars.

Makes 36 bars

The Silver Cobwebs

A German Folktale as told by Robert O. Day

ONCE upon a time, a long time ago, in a far away place, there lived a Spinster Spider all alone on a web high over the drapes in one corner of the living room. Only once each year at Christmas time, just before the Christmas tree is put up, did anyone pay any attention to her. That's when mother swished Spinster right out of her corner with a broom and made her hide in a hole. Then they brought in the tree and the whole family helped to decorate it and put presents under it.

On this Christmas eve Dusty the dog and Midnight the cat were allowed to come into the living room to see the tree.

"Isn't it beautiful, all green and covered with decorations," said Dusty. "It's too bad they can't have a Christmas tree all year long."

"Oh no, that would never do," explained Midnight, "No one would ever play with us if Christmas lasted all year long."

"They wouldn't, why?" asked Dusty.

"Because they would be all dressed up and acting good so they would be sure to get their Christmas presents." Midnight explained.

Spinster sat in her hole listening to Dusty and Midnight and feeling very sad because she had never seen a Christmas tree. Then she had an idea. If she found the Christmas Fairy, maybe she would be allowed to see the tree. So she crept slowly out of her hole and went looking for the fairy until she found her.

"Christmas Fairy," Spinster Spider explained, "I have never dared to come out of the hole and I do so want to. I would very much like to see, and maybe, please, touch the Christmas tree?"

"Poor Spinster, I know you must be very sad being left out of Christmas each year. That's not fair. This year you shall not only see the tree, but I will let you climb from limb to limb and see everything on the tree. Would that be a good Christmas present?"

"Oh yes, please! That will be wonderful!" said the spider.

So the Christmas fairy took the spider to the tree and left her on the top branch by the star. "I have to visit some children for a while," she said, "But you have a good time. Be sure to see everything."

After the fairy left, Spinster climbed from branch to branch and touched each ball, candy cane, and item on the tree. Just before it was time for the children to wake up the Christmas Fairy came to take Spinster home and saw an ugly, gray cobweb all over the tree.

"What happened to the tree" asked the fairy. And she was about to cry, because everywhere that Spinster had been she had left a cobweb.

"I'm sorry," said Spinster, "I was excited being able to see everything on the tree, I must have left my web on. I'm sorry! What shall we do, I hear the children coming."

"I know!" said the Christmas Fairy, "Here's what I'll do." Then she took her wand and touched the tree three times and turned all the ugly cobwebs into silver strands that hung from every limb.

All who saw the tree that year thought it was the most beautiful tree they had ever seen, especially Spinster, who was very happy because she now had a part in Christmas. From that time until this, every year people have continued to put silver tinsel on their Christmas trees.

3-D Mobile
Art Project/Decoration

MATERIALS LIST:

foam trays or foam plates
scissors
needle and thread
spool of ⅛ inch ribbon
cookie cutters
glue
glitter, beads, sequins, lace, ribbon, etc.
markers

INSTRUCTIONS:

1. Wash and dry used foam trays (or ask your butcher or produce manger for a couple of clean ones).

2. Cut sides off of trays or plates.

3. Place cookie cutter onto foam and press down hard to place designs into foam surface.

4. Cut designs out of foam. You need to keep the design simple in order to cut them out with scissors, if you want to get more elaborate you will have to use a utility knife.

5. To make the slit down the center of the ornament, on piece A draw line from the top to half way point, on piece B draw from bottom to half way point.

6. With scissors cut to the half way point. Now cut slit to 1/8 of an inch opening. Repeat with other piece.

7. Connect two pieces together by sliding slits until you have a good fit and bottom is flat.

8. With a needle and double thread, run needle through all three pieces at top of ornament. Pull thread through and knot well at desired length.

9. Decorate ornament anyway you choose. Color with markers. Glue, beads, gold braid, glitter, etc. Let dry.

10. Make at least six-eight ornaments depending on size of hoop.

11. Cut ribbon to different lengths. Tie and knot ribbon to inside of hoop.

12 Cut 2 pieces of 1/2 inch ribbon 24 inches long, tie them around inside of hoop at four equal places. Put hoop back together. At the center of the two 24 inch ribbons use a twist tie to create a loop for hanging up your mobile.

13. Tie ornaments onto 1/8 inch ribbon in 8 to 10 inch lengths.

14. Make small bows and attach to the bottom of each ribbon to hide knot.

15. Suspend mobile from ceiling, under a light fixture or near a doorway.

SUGGESTIONS:: You could just make these decorations for your tree or even use as place cards for a festive table decoration (if they have flat bottoms and will stand). Also you could add a large bow at the top where you hang it up and place a cluster of mistletoe for a kissing good time.

Fiesta Bravo

Chicken Enchiladas • Pinto Bean Casserole • Mexican Rice

Not Quite "Fried" Ice Cream

Chicken Enchiladas

"Better than Chili's. Such a creamy tasty filling. They are great."
Koko Mihilas - Food Taster

1	cup chicken broth
2	cups sour cream
2	cans cream of chicken soup
1	can diced green chilies
1	small onion diced
1	teaspoon chili powder
½	teaspoon salt
½	teaspoon garlic powder
¼	teaspoon thyme
1	8 ounce can sliced mushrooms (optional)
3	cups cooked and cubed or shredded chicken
⅓	pound grated cheese
1	package of 20 flour tortillas

Preheat oven to 350° F. Grease a 9 x 13 inch baking pan; set aside. Mix all the ingredients together except the chicken, cheese and tortillas. Remove 2½ cups of the mixture and put aside to be used on top of enchiladas. To the remaining mixture add the two cups of chicken. Place ¼ cup of chicken mixture in each tortilla and roll up. Put into baking pan. When all the tortillas are filled and placed into the pan pour the 2 cups of sauce on top of enchiladas and sprinkle with the cheese. Bake for 25 minutes or until cheese is melted.

Makes 14-18 servings

Pinto Bean Casserole

"Really good and spicy" Brenda Allen -Kitchen Tester

2	tablespoons vegetable oil
1	medium onion, chopped
1	medium red bell pepper, chopped
2	garlic cloves, minced
½	teaspoon dried oregano
1	(7 ounce) can chopped green chilies
1	cup thick and chunky salsa
2	(15 ounce) cans chili-seasoned pinto beans, undrained
1	cup shredded Cheddar cheese

Preheat oven to 350° F. In a large pot heat oil over medium heat. Add onion, red bell pepper, garlic and oregano and cook, stirring, until vegetables begin to soften, about 4 to 5 minutes. Add chopped green chilies, salsa, and beans with their sauce. Bring to a boil, stirring. Pour all ingredients into a lightly greased 2 quart casserole dish. Scatter cheese on top. Bake in preheated oven for 25 minutes, or until beans are bubbly and cheese is melted. Serve hot.

Makes 6 Servings

Mexican Rice

1	carrot, peeled and cut into 1/4-inch dice
2	tablespoons vegetable oil
2	cups long-grain white rice
1	medium onion, chopped
3	garlic cloves, minced
½	teaspoon ground cumin
¾	cup canned pureed tomatoes
1	(14 1/2-ounce) can chicken broth
¼	teaspoon pepper

In a small saucepan of boiling salted water, cook carrot until just tender, about 3 minutes. Drain and rinse under cold running water; drain well.

In a large saucepan, heat oil over medium heat. Add rice and cook, stirring, about 1 minute to coat with oil. Stir in onion and garlic. Cook, stirring until onion is translucent, about 3 minutes.

Stir in cumin, tomatoes, chicken broth, pepper, and 1 cup water. Bring to a boil. Reduce heat to low, cover and cook 15 to 18 minutes or until liquid is absorbed and rice is tender. Remove from heat and let stand 5 minutes. Add cooked carrot and stir gently to combine. Serve hot.

Makes 8 -10 Servings

VARIATION: This Mexican Rice is the mild type of rice you get in a Mexican restaurant. To make this already good rice into Spanish Rice add 1 cup medium salsa, 1 tablespoon chili powder and 1 green pepper diced. Then to serve: put a pile of crushed tortilla chips on your plate; add a good pile of rice on top of chips and sprinkle with shredded cheese. Yum!

Not Quite "Fried" Ice Cream

2 teaspoons margarine
2 tablespoons brown sugar
½ teaspoons cinnamon
⅔ cup bran flakes (without raisins,) crushed to 1/2 cup
2⅔ cups vanilla ice-cream

Melt margarine in small saucepan; remove from heat. Stir in brown sugar and cinnamon; blend well. Stir in cereal. Form ice milk into 4 balls. Roll in cereal mixture to coat (I like using my hands better). Cover; freeze. Let stand at room temperature a few minutes before serving.

Makes 4 Servings

Suggestions: Any flavor of ice cream or frozen yogurt can be substituted. Try serving a scoop of "fried" ice cream in a small bowl with a puddle of chocolate sauce, caramel sauce, or a tablespoon of hot spiced apples.

Letter of Thanks

Author unknown

On the first day of Christmas my true love gave to me.
A Partridge in a Pear Tree.

My Darling John:

I answered the door today and to my delightful surprise the postman handed me a partridge in a pear tree. What a marvelous gift. I Just couldn't have been more surprised and pleased.

With deepest love and affection. Your only true love.

Agnes

On the second day of Christmas my true love gave to me.
Two turtle doves ...

Dearest John:

Again today the postman brought me a beautiful gift from you. Just imagine—two turtle doves. I'm so delighted. Your gift is so thoughtful. They're absolutely adorable.

All my love,

Agnes

On the third day of Christmas my true love gave to me.
Three French hens ...

My Dear, Dear John:

Aren't you the extravagant one. Now I really must protest. I don't deserve such generosity. Three French Hens. They're darling. But I must insist, you've been far too kind.

Lovingly,

Agnes

On the fourth day of Christmas my true love gave to me.
Four calling birds ...

My Dear Sweetheart:

Today again the postman knocked on my door and this time he delivered four calling birds. Now really John.
They're beautiful, but don't you think enough is enough? You're just being too romantic.

Affectionately,

Agnes

On the fifth day of Christmas my true love gave to me.
Five golden rings ...

My Dear Sweet John:

What an absolutely wonderful surprise. Today the postman brought me five golden rings. One for each finger.
You're just impossible, but I love it. Frankly, all those birds are beginning to get on my nerves.

With love,

Agnes

On the sixth day of Christmas my true love gave to me.
Six geese a laying ...

Dear John:

When I opened the door this morning there were six geese a-laying on my front steps. So you're back to the birds again. John they're huge! Where in the world will I keep them, or what will I do with all those eggs they're a-laying? The neighbors are complaining about all the noise and the smell and I can't sleep a wink. Please, please stop.

Cordially,

Agnes

On the seventh day of Christmas my true love gave to me.
Seven swans a swimming ...

Dear John:

What's with you and all these blasted birds? Now it's seven swans a-swimming. What kind of lousy joke is this? Bird droppings all over the house. My fingers are raw to the bone from building all these bird cages. I can't sleep. It's not funny any longer so stop it immediately.

    Sincerely,

    Agnes

On the eighth day of Christmas my true love gave to me.
Eight maids a-milking...

OK, Buster.

What in the world is going on? What in Sam Hill am I going to do with eight maids a-milking? I prefer the birds. It's not enough with all those birds and maids, they had to bring all their cows with them. The lawn is a mess. You have to be careful where you step, and the house smells awful. I'm warning you— lay off.

    Most Sincerely,

    Agnes

On the ninth day of Christmas my true love gave to me.
Nine pipers piping ...

Hey Jerk,

What are you, some kind of weirdo? Today there's nine pipers piping. All they do is chase the maids. The cows are giving too much milk. The neighbors refuse to buy the milk. The birds are all screeching because of the playing pipers and the maids refuse to eat goose eggs. What am I supposed to do? The neighbors have started eviction proceedings against me. I'll get you.

    With lasting Hatred,

    Agnes

*On the tenth day of Christmas my true love gave to me.
Ten ladies dancing ...*

You rotten knucklehead.

Now there's ten ladies dancing. All they do is dance all night long. I don't have enough food storage to last very many more days. They're eating me out of house and home. All the cows are getting sick, all the milk is going sour, and the Board of Health is threatening to condemn the place. I've had it, you stupid blockhead. I'm siccing the police on you.

One who means it,

Agnes

*On the eleventh day of Christmas my true love gave to me.
Eleven Lords a-leaping ...*

Listen you Goon.

What's with eleven Lords a-leaping? All those maids and ladies and pipers are driving me nuts. All twenty-three of the birds have been trampled to death. I hope you're satisfied.

Your sworn enemy,

Agnes

*On the twelfth day of Christmas my true love gave to me.
Twelve drummers drumming ...*

Dear Sir:

This is to acknowledge your latest gift of twelve drummers drumming which you have seen fit to inflict upon my client. Miss McFurry's destruction was of course total, and she is now at Happydale Sanitarium where attendants have instructions to shoot you on sight.

Enclosed, please find a bill for all damages and a warrant for your arrest.

Yours truly,

G.F. Bailey

Attorney at Law

Fabric Basket
Art Project

MATERIALS AND CUTTING LIST:

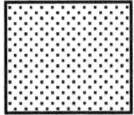

1 - 8 inch square of batting
2 - 8 inch squares fabric (1 of each coordinated prints)

2- 2¼ x 10 inch strip (1 of each fabrics)
1 - 2¼ x 10 inch strip of batting

4 - ¼ x 14 inch satin ribbon
thread the color of ribbon

INSTRUCTIONS:

1. Cut two squares of fabric, each 8 inches square. That is one fabric for the inside, one for the outside, and the same size square of batting for the middle.

2. Cut 2 strips of fabric for the handle (2¼ x 10 inch) and the same size batting.

Handle Sandwich
(batting, outside, inside)

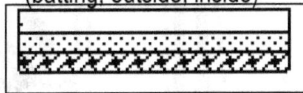

3. To make the handle sew the two strips right sides together, then add the layer of batting. Sew all three pieces together using a ¼ inch seam allowance on each side. Now turn and press. For added stability top stitch ½ inch from each edge. Set handle aside.

4. To make body of basket: On the outside fabric mark the center on two sides. Now lay the handle (outside fabric down) on the spots you marked as center and pin in place. Lay remaining square of fabric right sides together and place batting on top. Sew ¼ inch seam on all four sides leaving an opening on one side large enough to turn. Turn right side out. Press.

5. Finally add the ribbon. Pin ribbon in place about 2 inches from each side leaving a tail of about 3 inches off each edge (see diagram 3 for placement layout). Then zig-zag over ribbon (Make sure not to sew over the handle). Sew down all four pieces of ribbon.

6. Next whipstitch the opening closed.

7. Tie ribbons at corner and viola you have a cloth basket that you can fill with any type of goodie you want. This basket can be made in any number of sizes and is reversible.

Outside and
handle placement

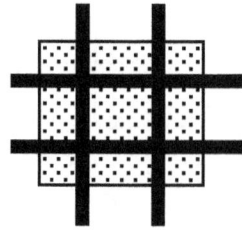

Ribbon placement

Nutty Caramel Corn

"Reminds me of Cracker Jacks only better." Jared Day

6	quarts popped popcorn
2	cups brown sugar, firmly packed
¼	cup molasses
¼	cup light corn syrup
½	cup butter or margarine
¼	teaspoon cream of tartar
1	teaspoon salt
1	teaspoon baking soda
2	cups lightly salted peanuts

Preheat oven to 250°F. Place popcorn in a large, 4-inch deep, buttered baking pan. Keep warm in oven. Cut large pieces of wax paper to fit cookie sheet. Lightly butter the wax paper. In a large saucepan, combine brown sugar, corn syrup, molasses, butter, cream of tartar and salt. Bring to a boil over medium-high heat, stirring constantly. Continue to stir constantly and boil rapidly until mixture reaches 260°F on a candy thermometer, about 5 minutes. Remove from heat. Add peanuts and mix. Stir in baking soda quickly but thoroughly. Remove popcorn from oven, place in a large paper grocery sack. Pour syrup mixture over popcorn. Stir gently until well coated. Bake at 200°F for 1 hour, stirring 2 or 3 times during baking. Turn over at once onto wax paper. Spread out and allow to cool completely. Break or cut apart. Store in tightly covered container.

Makes 6 quarts.

Gift Suggestion: Decorate brown lunch bags in any method you want. Fill bag with Nutty Caramel Corn. Fold top of bag over and punch two holes through all layers. Then thread ribbon through holes and tie a bow or put a candy cane through holes to close. Give to your favorite popcorn eater.

I Held the Christ Child

MyLinda Butterworth

ONCE upon a lowly hill
A star did rise
And it shown oh so bright.
I was but a shepherdess meek
And did see its light
An angel appeared
and spoke to us words
of joy and celebration,
that Christ the Lord was born this day
in the city of David.
My heart did leap with joy
at this announcement,
A Saviour had been born,
Born to be the Light of the world,
Born to show us the way back to God.
I felt so unworthy to be in the presence of
one so omnipotent,
But how I wanted to see the newborn king.

My brothers and I followed the star
and listened to the words of the angels.
Soon we came to a humble stable
wherein the infant child lay.
Mary, his young mother nestled her tiny child
to her bosom and hummed a gentle lullaby,
He smiled and cooed,
and the radiance that surrounded him
filled me with awe.
I fell to my knees, bowed my head
and thanked God for this tiny gift.
Mary came over to me and lifted my head,

She smiled and then placed
her son in my arms.
His eyes looked into mine and I knew
that **he** was the Son of God,
for his gaze filled my heart
with peace and understanding,
the likes of which I have never known before.

Tears welled in my eyes
as I held the tiny king tight.
I took my shawl and wrapped it around him
to shelter him from the chill of the night.
Teardrops rolled down my cheeks
and fell on his little face,
He smiled at me.
The love I felt from this wee child
made my heart swell,
I wanted to sing with the angels
that this is the king of kings,
here to fulfill the prophesies of old.
And that I, a young shepherdess was
privileged to hold him close to my heart.
I stood and gave the boy child
back to his mother,
I smiled and she touched my cheek.
She then cradled him in her arms
and gently rocked him to sleep.

As my brothers and I left,
I turned back to see
a father, mother and a babe
standing in a stable,
A light shining brightly over
the place where they dwelled
and the heavens filled with music
sung by scores of angels.

I took all that I had seen
and stored them in my heart.
I had held the Christ child
in my arms that special night,
But would always carry his light in my heart.

Linda S. Day ©

Rag Angel
Art Project

MATERIALS LIST:

1 yard of printed fabric for body
8 inch square of muslin for face
2 inch styrofoam ball
batting (optional)
spanish moss or yarn
ribbon
miniature wreath for halo
ribbons, button
low melt glue gun
scissors

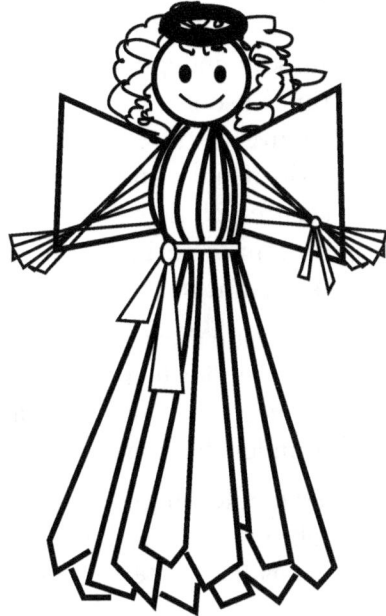

INSTRUCTIONS:

1. Fold your yard of fabric in half, selvage edges together and either cut, rotary cut or tear the fabric into one inch strips from selvage to selvage.

2. Stack up all your strips, unfolded. Take away about 5-6 strips to make the arms and set aside. Also set 2-3 strips aside for tying purposes.

3. Gather up all the strips together in one and hand and find the middle. When you have found the middle take one strip that you set aside for tying and tie a knot around the center of all the strips, cut off, set aside.

4. To make arms take the five strips you set aside, cut each strip in half, then half again. Stack them up and tie either end with scrap fabric to create arms and hands, set aside.

5. To create head, take the knotted section of the body and place on top of styrofoam ball. Spread all the rags over the ball until completely

covered. Then take a rag scrap and tie directly under the doll's "chin" to create it's head.

Body.

Arms

is

6. Take muslin fabric scrap place over head. Work with the fabric until one side smooth enough to paint a face on it. (I sometimes use scrap of batting under the muslin to give a stuffed head look) Find you scrap strip of fabric and wrap around the neck until secure and tie off. Trim excess muslin from bottom of neck, use glue gun to secure face fabric if it starts to slide.

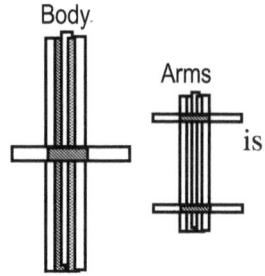

7. To create the body separate all the loose rag strips under head in half and place arms in between the rags. Take a final strip and tie it under the arms to create a waist.

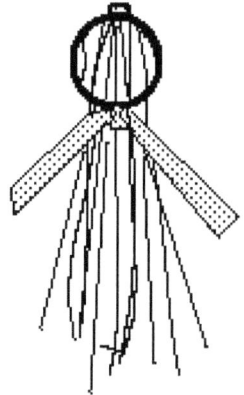

8. To create wings sew or hot glue a square of fabric with a little batting in between to make wings. Tie center of wings with either ribbon or rag to create the look of wings. Hot glue wings to center of back.

9. To finish your rag angel glue on Spanish moss for hair, buttons for eyes and a small wreath for a halo. Add a small piece of lace around neck to cover raw edges and glue glitter on wings (optional). Please note that if you are making this for a small child you will have to sew on buttons, wings, and use yarn for hair.

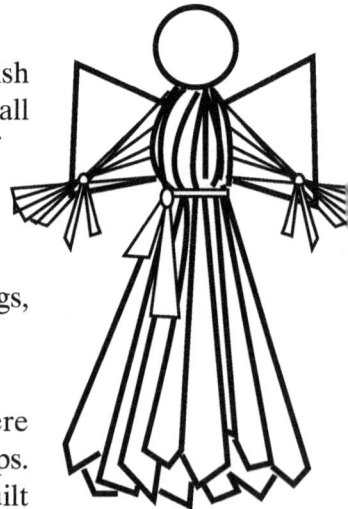

NOTE: This is a pioneer craft. These dolls were originally made from rags or leftover fabric scraps. The heads were stuffed with leftover rags or quilt batting, their hair was yarn and quite often they didn't have faces unless there were buttons to be found or berries to stain their faces.

Milky Way Cake

"Simply out of this world" J.L. - Kitchen Tester

8	Milky Way candy bars
1	cup margarine
2	cups sugar
4	eggs
2½	cups flour
½	teaspoon baking soda
1½	cup buttermilk
1	cup pecans

Preheat oven to 325° F. In a heavy pot melt candy bars and ½ cup margarine over low heat. In a bowl cream sugar and other ½ cup of margarine. Add eggs alternately with buttermilk. Add flour and baking soda and mix. Add candy mixture, milk and pecans. Bake in a greased and floured bundt or angel food cake pan at for 1 hour and 20 minutes. When cool remove from pan and dust with powdered sugar or drizzle with a chocolate glaze.

VARIATION: For a little fun try using snickers bars instead of Milky Way bars and omit the nuts. The cake won't be quite as moist but equally as delicious.

Serves 12-16

The Legend of the Christmas Robin

As told by Linda Weaver Day

"Now my little child, let me tell you the *Legend of the Christmas Robin*, and how he got his red breast." Grandfather Burkey said, as I crawled upon his lap. "When I was a boy, no bigger than you, my grandfather told me this story from the old country.

Once upon a time, in a Holy land of high hills and green valleys, there was in the little town called Bethlehem, that had unexpectedly become full of people. The reason so many were in the town was that the Roman governor ordered everyone to go to the town they were born in to be taxed. People had come from everywhere down the dusty trails, walking or riding animals, and they were all looking for a place to sleep.

Behind one Inn, that was especially quiet with cool water in the well and shady trees to keep the hot sun from the courtyard, was a stable. And in the stable there were many different kinds of animals that waited while their masters were in the Inn. As they were all God's creatures, and were friendly beasts, they talked to one another about their travels and their masters until the sun had gone down, and a chill began to fill the air. Then weary with their labors of the day, the beasts in the stable settled down to rest.

A little brown robin, that had been outside on the roof, suddenly flew inside the stable and perching himself on the railing. "The night is here, the night is here, but the cloak of darkness does not cover the sky. There is a bright star in the heavens," he said," and look! Oh! Look! It shines brightest here on our little stable."

And as the animals looked, the light got brighter and brighter and an angel appeared from the heavens and said, "It is time for the Prince of Peace to be born. Tonight, in your little stable, you will be present when the Savior of the world is born. Even now, Joseph leads a donkey carrying Mary on it's back, she will be his mother." As the animals watched the angel ascend into the heavens, they noticed how extra brightly the stars in the heavens twinkled.

Then a silhouette of Joseph was at the door of the stable. As he lit a lantern and hung it from the rafter, the weary faces of Mary and Joseph reflected the long hours they had been on the road. Then Joseph spread his coat over the fresh hay and helped Mary down from the donkey, so she could rest on it. Mary's sweet face was filled with anxiety for the coming birth of her baby.

Joseph led their donkey into a stall, and did all he could to make things ready for the baby's birth. He had hoped for a better place for this special child to be born, but it was the fulfillment of prophecy.

" Ohhhhhhh! Ahhhhh! sighed the animals, as the wee babe was born.

"Heee Haaaaw, Heee Haaaw. Up! Up the hills and down I have traveled the dusty roads with this fair maiden upon my back. I am not weary for my deeds, for I know that I carried a King and his mother." The shaggy haired donkey gently brayed with a sigh, then blinked his eyes and swished his tail, as he munched on the hay in his stall.

The flutter of wings and the soft voice of the little brown robin was heard. "And what have we to give the King of Kings this Holy night?" The animals looked at the wee babe, now wrapped in swaddling clothes, and each spoke of what his gift to the Christ Child would be.

"Moooo Moooo, My new hay and this manger will I give him, to be his first cradle. The hay to pillow his head." And the black and white cow nuzzled her nose against the pile of fresh hay piled in the corner of the stable.

"Baaaa Baaaa. My wool is soft and will cradle the Babe as He lies in the manger." And her pink little nose pushed the lambs wool to the feet of Joseph, who lined the manger of straw with the soft lambs wool. Then Mary gently laid little Baby Jesus in the manger.

"Coooo Cooooo." said the doves from the rafters, high in the stable, "We will coooo a lullaby, that this blessed baby will not cry. Coooooo Cooooo," they sang, as their heads nodded back and forth .

"Hummmph" said the camel, all surly and brown, as he shuffled his big feet on the ground. "I shall carry the gift of the Wise Men to this King of Kings one day." Hummmph.. Hummmph..Hummmmph..now note what I say."

And the robin cocked his head sprightly to one side and said, "Oh, what have I to give to the Babe in the manger? I have no soft wool like the sheep for him to lay on. The hay in the manger is not mine to give like the black and white cow. I could not carry them on my wings over the great hills as the shaggy haired donkey did, nor could I bring the Wise Men to this King with their gifts, as the stately camel." Sadly the little brown robin hopped over to the side of the small fire that Joseph had made to keep the chill of the night from his little family.

Fluttering his wings to smooth his feathers, the fire suddenly glowed warmer and brighter. "Yes! That's it!" said the little robin excitedly, "I shall flutter my wings here at the fires edge, so that the Babe in the manger will stay warm through the night. That will be my gift!"

And so the little brown robin fanned the fire with his wings all through the night. In the morning, as the sunlight beamed brightly into the stable, the animals all awoke.

"Baaaa, Baaaa. Wake up little robin!", but he little robin just lay lifeless beside the glowing embers of the fire. The feathers on his breast were singed black from fanning the fire all night. His gift to the Babe in the manger of warmth on that first Christmas night, had been the willing gift of his life. When Joseph found the little brown robin and understood what he had done, he put him in his hand and gently stroked his head.

So touched by the little robin's unselfish gift, the Christ Child granted him a covering of red on his breast where it had been scorched, as a sign forever more of his love and sacrifice that first Christmas night. As the sun again broke through the clouds, the little robin redbreast stirred. Then he sat up and flew from Joseph's hand to the edge of the manger, where he cocked his head and ruffled his new red feathers. The Baby Jesus in the manger smiled and reached His hand up to the robin, as he flew high into the clouds toward heaven.

The animals looked at each other and nodded, remembering all that had happened that Holy night, in the humble stable behind the Inn at the bend of the road in Bethlehem. And today, we also remember the gift of the animals whenever we see a little Robin Redbreast hopping across the grass, perched in a tree tending its' nest, or flying high in the clouds toward heaven.

Remember the legend of the little Robin Redbreast, my child, and tell it to your children and grandchildren one day.

Christmas Ornaments for Birds
Outdoor Decoration

MATERIALS LIST:

Pinecones
wild bird seed
peanut butter
plastic bag
red or yellow yarn
orange
suet (the fat drippings)
wild bird seed
sunflower seeds
berries optional

INSTRUCTIONS:

PROJECT 1:

1. With your fingers or a butter knife spread peanut butter over entire surface of the pinecone.

2. In a plastic bag put 1/2 cup of wild bird seed.

3. Drop pinecone into bag and press birdseed into peanut butter, until well coated.

4. Tie on a piece of bright yarn to top of pinecone and hang in tree and watch the birds have a holiday feast.

5. Repeat process until you've made as many pinecone feeders as you want.

PROJECT 2:

1. Cut orange in half. Scoop or peel out the fruit leaving a orange bowl. (Don't forget to eat the sweet orange, it's your treat)

2. Pierce three holes in orange peel, 1/2 inch below edge.

3. Cut yarn into three 8 inch pieces. Tie knot in one end of each piece, thread through hole in orange. Gather all threads together and knot at top.

4. Mix suet with wild bird seeds and sunflower seeds.

5. Fill orange half with seed mixture then hang on tree branch and watch the birds from your window. Identify the different birds that come to the buffet.

NOTE: Don't forget to take your cranberry and popcorn strings and hang them in the trees after you've taken down your Christmas tree for a New Year celebration of life.

Hummingbird Cake

I have never had anything so GOOD! It was Delicious!
Erin Potter - Kitchen Tester

5	cups flour
2	cups sugar
1	teaspoon baking soda
1	teaspoon salt
1	teaspoon cinnamon
3	eggs beaten
1½	cup oil
1½	teaspoon vanilla
1	12 oz. can crushed pineapple, undrained
1	cup pecans or walnuts, chopped
2	cups chopped bananas

Grease and flour (3) round 9 inch cake pans or one large layer pan and set aside. Combine flour, sugar, soda, salt and cinnamon in a large bowl; add eggs and oil stirring until all dry ingredients are moistened. Do not beat. Stir in vanilla, pineapple, nuts and bananas. Make sure batter is blended well, but don't beat. Spoon batter into pans, bake at 350° for 25 to 30 minutes. Cool for 10 minutes in pan, remove from pans, let cool completely. Frost with Cream Cheese Frosting and sprinkle with 1 cup of chopped nuts.

Cream Cheese Frosting

1	8 oz package cream cheese, softened
½	cup butter/margarine, softened
1	pound powdered sugar
1	teaspoon vanilla

Combine cream cheese and butter and mix until smooth. Add box of powdered sugar and vanilla, beat until light and fluffy. Makes enough frosting to cover a 3 layer cake.

The Festival of St. Nicholas
from Hans Brinker, or The Silver Skates
by Mary Mapes Dodge

Christmas Day is devoted by the Hollanders to church rites and pleasant family visiting. It is on Saint Nicholas' Eve that their young people become half wild with joy and expectation. To some of them it is a sorry time, for the saint is very candid, and if any of them have been bad during the past year, he is quite sure to tell them so. Sometimes he carries a birch rod under his arm and advises the parents to give them scoldings in place of confections, and floggings instead of toys.

It was well that the boys hastened to their abodes on that bright winter evening, for in less than an hour afterward, the saint made his appearance in half the homes of Holland. He visited the king's palace and in the self-same moment appeared in Annie Bouman's comfortable home. Probably one of our silver half dollars would have purchased all that his saintship left at the peasant Bouman's; but a half dollar's worth will sometimes do for the poor what hundreds of dollars may fail to do for the rich; it makes them happy and grateful, fills them with new peace and love.

Hilda van Gleck's little brothers and sisters were in a high state of excitement that night. They had been admitted into the grand parlor; they were dressed in their best, and had been given two cakes apiece at supper. Hilda was as joyous as any. Why not? Saint Nicholas would never cross a girl of fourteen from his list, just because she was tall and looked almost like a woman. on the contrary, he would probably exert himself to do honor to such an august-looking damsel. Who could tell? So she sported and laughed and danced as gaily as the youngest, and was the soul of all their merry games. Father, mother and grandmother looked on approvingly; so did grandfather, before he spread his large red handkerchief over his face, leaving only the top of his skullcap visible. This kerchief was his ensign of sleep.

Earlier in the evening all had joined in the fun. In the general hilarity there had seemed to be a difference only in bulk between grandfather and the baby. Indeed a shade of solemn expectation, now and then flitting across the faces of the younger members, had made them seem rather more thoughtful than their elders.

Now the spirit of fun reigned supreme. The very flames danced and capered in the polished grate. A pair of prim candles that had been starring at the astral lamp began to wink at other candles far away in the mirrors. There was a long bellrope suspended from the ceiling in the corner, made of glass beads netted over a cord nearly as thick as your wrist. It generally hung in the shadow and made no sign; but tonight it twinkled from end to end. Its handle of crimson glass sent reckless dashes of red at the papered wall, turning its dainty blue stripes into purple. Passers-by halted to catch the merry laughter floating, through curtain and sash, into the street, then skipped on their way with a startled consciousness that the village was wide awake. At last matters grew so uproarious that the grandsire's red kerchief came down from his face with a jerk. What decent old gentleman could sleep in such a racket! Mynheer van Gleck regarded his children with astonishment. The baby even showed symptoms of hysterics. It was high time to attend to business. Madame suggested that if they wished to see the good Saint Nicholas they should sing the same loving invitation that had brought him the year before.

The baby stared and thrust his fist into his mouth as Mynheer put him down upon the floor. Soon he sat erect, and looked with a sweet scowl at the company. With his lace and embroideries, and his crown of blue ribbon and whalebone (for he was not quite past the tumbling age), he looked like the king of babies.

The other children, each holding a pretty willow basket, formed at once in a ring, and moved slowly around the little fellow, lifting their eyes, meanwhile, for the saint to whom they were about to address themselves was yet in mysterious quarters.

Madame commenced playing softly upon the piano, soon the voices rose—gentle, youthful voices—rendered all the sweeter for their tremor:

> "Welcome, friend! Saint Nicholas, welcome!
> Bring no rod for us, tonight!
> While our voices bid thee, welcome,
> Every heart with joy is light.

> Tell us every fault and failing,
> We will bear thy keenest railing,
> So we sing—so we sing—
> Thou shalt tell us everything!

"Welcome, friend! Saint Nicholas, welcome!
Welcome to this merry band!
Happy children greet thee, welcome!
Thou art glad'ning all the land!

Fill each empty hand and basket,
'Tis thy little ones who ask it,
So we sing—so we sing—
Thou wilt bring us everything!

During the chorus, sundry glances, half in eagerness, half in dread, had been cast toward the polished folding doors. Now a loud knocking was heard. The circle was broken in an instant. Some of the little ones, with a strange mixture of fear and delight, pressed against their mother's knee. Grandfather bent forward, with his chin resting upon his hand; grandmother lifted her spectacles; Mynheer van Gleck, seated by the fireplace slowly drew his meerschaum from his mouth, while Hilda and the other children settled themselves beside him in an expectant group.

The knocking was heard again.

"Come in," said madame softly.

The door slowly opened, and Saint Nicholas, in full array, stood before them.

You could have heard a pin drop!

Soon he spoke. What a mysterious majesty in his voice! what kindliness in his tones!

"Karel van Gleck, I am pleased to greet thee, and they honored vrouw Katherine, and they son and his good vrouw Annie!"

"Children, I greet ye all! Hendrick, Hilda, Broom, Katy, Huygens, and Lucretia! And they cousins, Wolfert, Diedrich, Mayken, Voost and Katrina! Good children ye have been, in the main, since I last accosted ye. Diedrich was rude at Haarlem fair last fall, but he has tried to atone for it since. Mayken has failed of late in her lessons, and too many sweets and trifles have gone to her lips, and two few coins to her charity box. Diedrich, I trust, will be a polite, manly boy for the future and Mayken will endeavor to shine as a student. Let her remember, too, that economy and thrift are needed in the foundation of a worthy and generous life. Little Katy has been cruel to the cat more than once. Saint Nicholas can hear the cat cry when its tail is pulled. I will forgive her if she will remember

from this hour that the smallest dumb creatures have feelings and must not be abused."

As Katy burst into a frightened cry, the saint graciously remained silent until she was soothed.

"Master Broom," he resumed, "I warn thee that boys who are in the habit of putting snuff upon the foot stove of the schoolmistress may one day be discovered and receive a flogging—But thou art such an excellent scholar, I shall make thee no further reproof.

"Thou, Hendrick, didst distinguish thyself in the archery match last spring, and hit the Doel, though the bird was swung before it to unsteady thine eye. I give thee credit for excelling in many sport and exercise—though I must not unduly countenance thy boat racing since it leaves thee too little time for thy proper studies.

"Lucretia and Hilda shall have a blessed sleep tonight. The consciousness of kindness to the poor, devotion in their souls, and cheerful, hearty obedience to household rule will render them happy.

"With one and all I avow myself well content. Goodness, industry, benevolence and thrift have prevailed in your midst. Therefore, my blessing upon you—and may the New Year find all treading the paths of obedience, wisdom and love. Tomorrow you shall find more substantial proofs that I have been in your midst. Farewell!"

With these words came a great shower of sugarplums, upon a line sheet spread out in front of the doors. A general scramble followed. The children fairly tumbled over each other in their eagerness to fill their baskets. Madame cautiously held the baby down in their midst, till the chubby little fists were filled. Then the bravest of the youngsters sprang and burst open the closed doors—in vain they peered into the mysterious apartment—Saint Nicholas was nowhere to be seen.

Santa Jar or Wise Man Jar
Art Activity/Gift Idea

MATERIALS LIST:

*Small jar with lid (baby food jars are what
we used)
gold gift wrap
buttons, beads, pearls, jewels, glitter
pom poms
fake fur, cotton balls felt
6x6"scrap of fabric for hat/ 12" for wise
man
low melt glue gun
scissors*

INSTRUCTIONS:

1. Lay 6x6 inch piece of fabric out and from the top left corner measure out to form a five inch (¼ of what would be a 10" circle). Be sure to measure the outside of the lid if you choose different jars. Allow ½ inch seam overlay for gluing.

2. Start gluing the outside curve of the circle to the lid. The straight edges are the seam from the top to the lid, glue them together. (For the wise man gather the outside of 10" ½ circle piece of fabric and glue to lid. Stuff slightly and glue down. Cut a 7 inch crown from gold wrapping paper and glue securely)

3. Finish the face by gluing on beard and mustache (use felt, fake fur or cotton balls). Then use felt (or construction paper) to make nose, eyes and eyebrows.

5. Add trim like a pom pom on the end of Santa's hat or jewels on the crown, etc.

6. Fill jar with candy or small gifts.

eye brows

moustache

eyes

nose

Santa beard

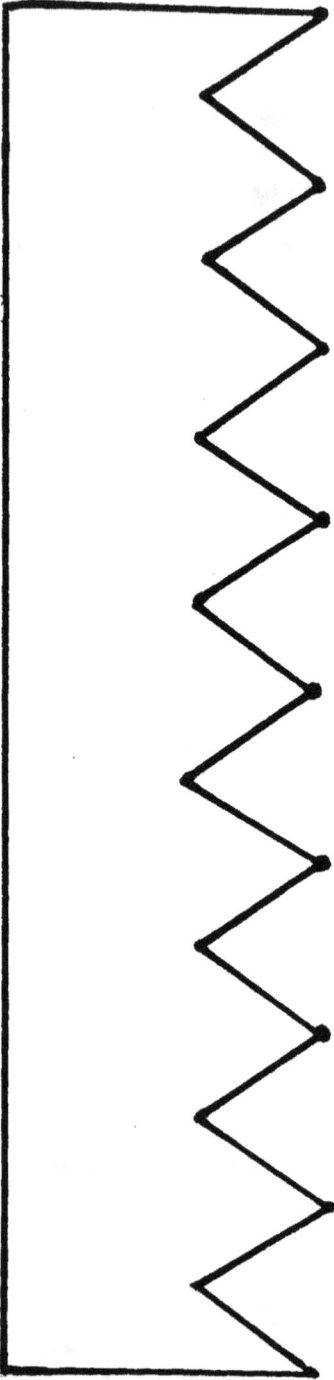

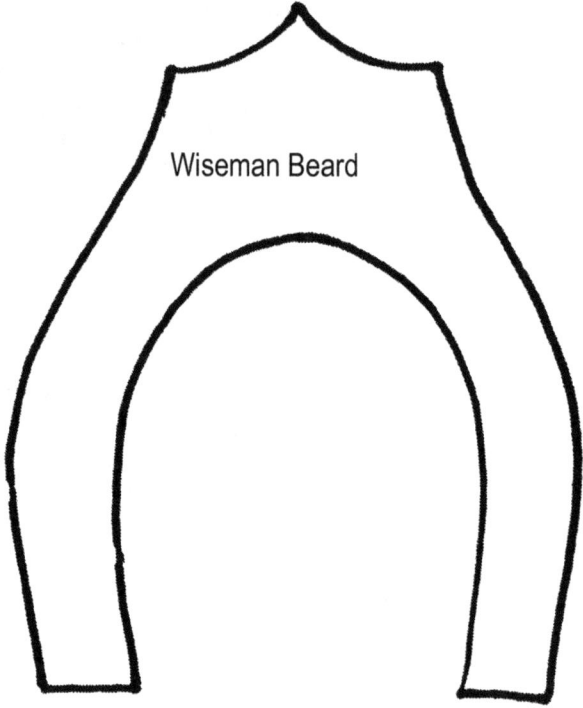

Wiseman Beard

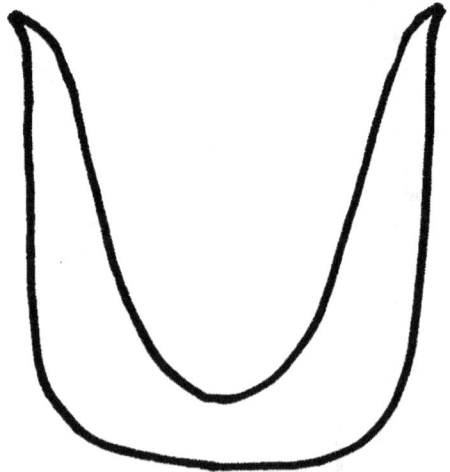

moustache

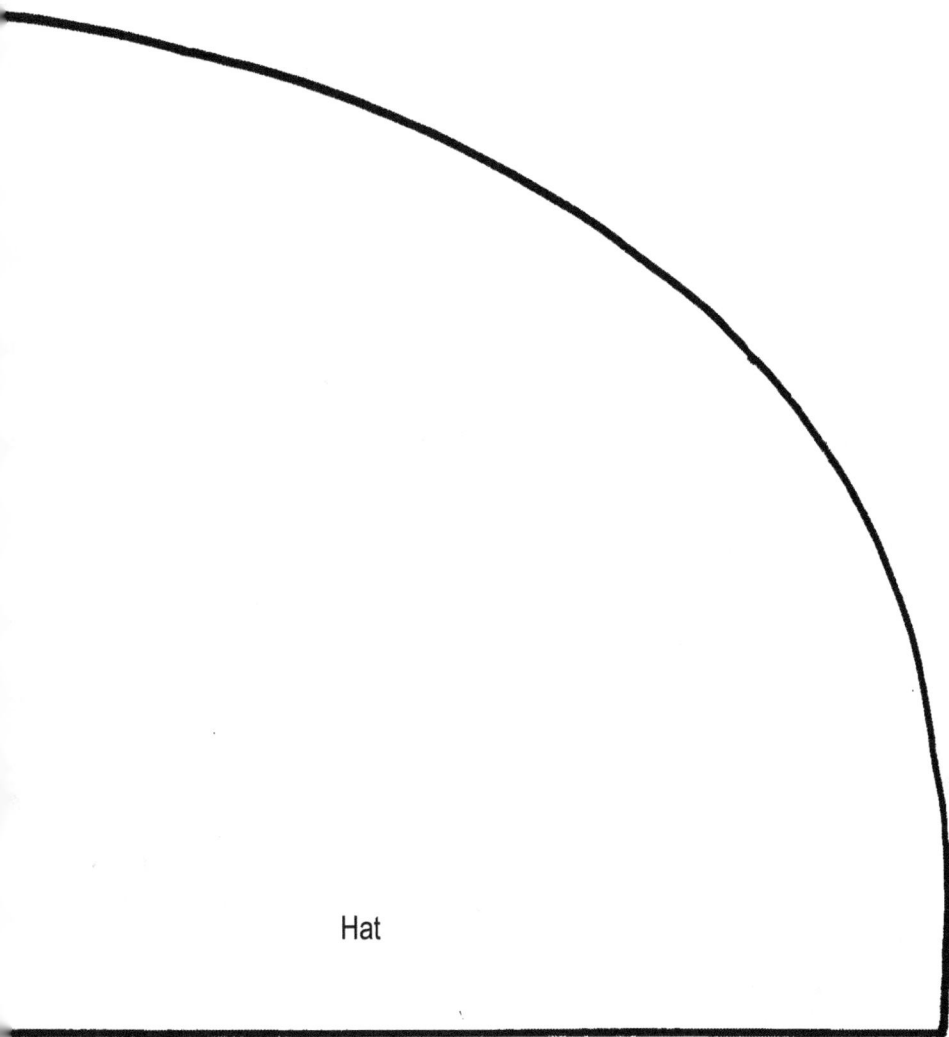

Hat

German Chocolate Pie

"Light, smooth and chocolaty. What more could I want?"
Linda Day - Kitchen Tester

½   pound of marshmallows (about 30-32 large)
    dash of salt
1   cup milk
1   teaspoon vanilla
2   cups whipped topping
½   cup coconut
½   cup semi-sweet chocolate chips
½   cup chopped pecans
1   baked 9" pie shell

In a large pot place marshmallows, chocolate and milk over medium heat, mix constantly until chocolate and marshmallows are melted. Remove from heat and mix in salt and vanilla, then set aside until cool. When cooled add coconut and nuts and mix, now gently fold in whipped topping and pour into pie shell. Chill for about 2 hours or until set (If chocolate mix is not completely cooled when nuts and coconut are added it will be lumpy and uneven). To serve top with a dollop of additional whipped topping and sprinkle with shaved chocolate.

Makes 8 servings

Variation: To turn this into a Peanut Butter Pie use the following: substitutes ½ cup peanut butter chips for chocolate chips, add a ¼ cup peanut butter and melt together with the marshmallows and milk. Then add ½ cup chopped peanuts in place of the pecans and eliminate the coconut. Follow the directions above and pour filling into a chocolate pie crust.

Poems for Christmas

Robert O. Day

Hurray! Hurray! For Christmas Day

Hurray! Hurray! for Christmas Day,
Hang mistletoe and holly.
So let it snow and north winds blow,
We're warm in the house, by golly!

Christmas is Coming – Santa's Getting Fat

Christmas is coming, Santa's getting fat,
Please drop a dollar in the poor man's hat;
If you haven't got a dollar, fifty cents will do,
If you haven't got fifty cents, come share my Christmas stew.

Making Cookies

In the bowl put chocolate bits, stir it round and round.
Next, an egg, three cups of flour - don't drop it on the ground.
Add some sugar, oil, and milk, and half a lid of 'neller -
Bake it up all nice and brown and give it to us fellers.

Wrapped Up Presents

There's lots of things at Christmas time that's lots of fun to do -
Eatin' stuff and buying things to name just one or two -
But when it comes to wrapped up gifts I wish every one was lazy.
All that guessing what's wrapped up inside - It almost drives me crazy!

Merry Christmas!!!!!!!!

God bless my Momma and My Dad
  My brothers and my Sis,
Who ne'er forget each Christmas day
  To give me each a gift.
But much more fun than getting them is giving to each one
Something great that they will like and have a lot of fun.
And if I pick it carefully -
  Being smart to do it right -
I can pick it up and play with it when they're all out of sight!
Merrrrry Christmas!!!!

Don't Eat Yulie!
Game/Family Entertainment

MATERIALS LIST:

Your favorite candy (M&M's, hard candies, chocolate assortment, etc.)
A copy of the game board on index weight paper
clear contact paper

INSTRUCTIONS:

Photocopy the game board on page 125 on a piece of index weight paper. Color in the pictures of Yulie in the nine blocks. Take a piece of clear contact paper and cover the game board for protection. (If you don't want to photocopy the game board then draw nine squares on a piece of index weight paper and draw, paste or create your own version of Yulie).

GAME INSTRUCTIONS:

Place one piece of candy in each square. Send one person out of the room while the group chooses one candy piece to be "YULIE". When the player returns he eats the candies one at a time. But the minute he touches "YULIE" the group yells "DON'T EAT YULIE"!! His turn is then over and the next player leaves the room. Continue until all have had a turn.

This is a great way to get rid of a lot of Christmas Candy!

Don't Eat Yulie!

Fill'er Up Soup

"A good hearty bowl of soup. My mouth watered the whole time it was cooking." Lisa Potter - Kitchen Tester

2	pounds lean ground beef
2	quarts water
1	cup celery
1	cup frozen corn
2	cups shredded cabbage
2	cups diced potatoes
2	cups stewed tomatoes
1	cup sliced carrots
2	onions diced
¼	cup rice
1½	teaspoons salt

Brown meat and drain; add water and bring to a full boil. Add vegetables and return to a boil. Add rice and season to taste. Simmer for 1 - 1½ hours. Makes a large hearty pot of soup.

Makes 12 large bowls full

Suggestion: If your in a hurry and want a good pot of thick hearty soup waiting for you at the end of the day, try putting all the ingredients in a crock pot on low.

Shaker Cheese Bread

"A good compliment to Fill'er Up Soup"

2	cups unbleached flour
1	teaspoon baking powder
¾	teaspoon salt
1½	teaspoons sugar
1	cup grated cheddar cheese (sharp cheddar is a good choice)
½	cup chopped onion (optional)
1	egg
¾	cup milk
2	tablespoons melted butter.

Preheat oven to 350° F. Blend the dry ingredients and mix in the cheese and onion. Beat the egg, milk and butter together and add to the dry ingredients. Stir just enough to blend. Let the batter stand for about 20 minutes. Pour into a greased, 5x9 inch loaf pan. Bake for 45 minutes to 1 hour.

Makes 1 loaf

Suggestion: For a herb and cheese bread, omit the onion and add 1 tablespoon of dill or caraway seeds.

Dad! Do I Hafta ?

Linda S. Day

IT was Christmas eve and our children, Mylinda 7; David 5; Gene 4 and Michael 3, were filled with all the anticipation of the past 24 days. The gifts under the little tree were almost overpowering in the front room. In some ways it was funny to see the packages multiply, but in another it was also very sad. You see, it soon turned into a competition between the grandparents to see who was going to provide the children with the most and best gifts. I don't have any idea how much money they spent that year, but it must have been a princely sum. The wrapping paper and bows alone would probably have paid our food bill for a month.

Every visit from the grandparents meant more gaily wrapped packages being placed under the Christmas tree, until there was no more room. Because the children were always wanting to go through the packages to shake them, squeeze them, and make guesses as to what was inside, we brought home two large tissue boxes from the grocery store, and we decorated them wrapping paper and placed a bow on one side, and started placing the presents in them. Soon they also were full and overflowing. Soon presents had began to multiply there too.

"Va", the children called out, as my Mother came in with her bag, She slept on the living room couch on every Christmas eve. With her camera at her side. She had already taken up several rolls of film on Christmas eve during the baking and frosting of Baby Jesus' Birthday cake; the reading of the Christmas story; and each child opening one present, as had been a family tradition.. As well as several pictures going down the hall to their bedrooms, the saying of evening prayers and now being tucked into bed. with giggles, tickles, hugs and kisses Now Va was going to be ready to take their pictures as they came back down the hall on Christmas morning.

Of course, since "Va" was spending the night on the couch, my husbands' parents had to be given the promise to be called ," as soon as the children got up", so they could be there before the gifts were opened. We agreed , but almost had a mutiny on our hands trying to get the children to wait, and just play with the gifts **we** had laid out for them.

Finally Grandpa and Grandma Day pulled into the driveway and hurried along the walk, up the steps, across the porch and dashed into the house. A place was made for them to sit and the "games began". I served as the one to take the gifts from their place under the tree and Daddy saw that they were handed to the right person. In order to not have any conflict in the opening process, each child was placed in a different area of the room, with grandparents for helpers. The gifts were piled up around them, and the stacks got higher and higher.

By the time the distribution job had been completed, it was nearly impossible to find the children for the pile of gifts surrounding them. It had taken all of 20 exciting minutes, but at least the tissue boxes were empty and all of the wrapping papers, etc. could be placed in them to help control some of the mess.

At Dad's signal ,"Okay kids' ! You may open your Christmas gifts." Eye sparkling with anticipation, everyone started opening their presents. Their little fingers struggling with the tape and ribbons and as fast as a gift was opened it was laid to the side, and Daddy or I picked up the trash and passed it over to be stuffed in one of the tissue boxes. After what seemed an eternity of furious package opening, the wrappings had disappeared from most of the presents, but the toys, clothes and "things" still kept the same barrier around each of the children. All the while this was going on the grandmas were snapping pictures and all the adults were giving out with appropriate 'Ooooohs" and "Aahhhhhh's" and "Isn't that nice?" 'Oh ! How cute" or "You can really use that." or "That will sure be useful [or fun]."

"Buzzzz! Buzzzzzz! went the doorbell" Look children, It is Great Grandpa and Grandma, and they have some presents for you." With that announcements our little 4 year old Gene climbed over one part of his mountain of gifts and struggled over to where his Daddy was standing. His red hair all tousled from the activities, he tugged on his Daddy's pants and shirt to get his attention.. Daddy bent over to see what he wanted, thinking he needed to get a drink of water, or ask if he could eat some more candy, instead, with his freckled little face as serious and sober as a judge, his little blues eyes filling with tears, and tension in his small body that looked like a bomb about to explode. Staring hard up at his Daddy, he whispered, "Daddy? Daddy, do I hafta' open any more presents? I'se tired!"

Somewhat amazed at his question, and working hard to control the urge to laugh, Daddy said, "Of course Gene! If you're tired of opening presents, what would you like to do?"

"Can I go outside and play on my trike or play with my cowboy gun?" he replied. "I don't want to have to open any more presents, O.K., Dad?"

Remembering when I was four, I was lucky to get one or two things for Christmas and here is our son with so many things that he just wants to play on his old trike or with his cowboy gun. "That really ought to be written up and sent in to Ripley's *Believe It Or Not*. ", I thought as his Daddy picked him up and hugged him with a big bear hug, like Daddy's do.

If that wasn't a big enough lesson about getting "too much of a good thing", the best part of this story come later after all of the children had gone outside to play. The women had moved to the kitchen to make the last preparations for the Christmas feast and the men relaxed to talk in peace and quiet for a while. It wasn't long, however, that I noticed a great deal of noise coming from the back yard. Since very few of the toys had left the "gift mountains" in the living room , we wondered what the children could be playing with that was stimulating so much fun and commotion. What could be causing all of the yelling, giggling and screaming.?

Going out the back door to investigate, we saw wrapping paper, bows, and all the things that had been stuffed into the decorated tissue boxes, scattered all over the yard.. Daddy had placed those boxes outside to give us a little more room, and the children had found them. With the creativity and imagination of youth they emptied them, and the boxes were now being used as barrels. Yes, they had became barrels of fun. The children had climbed inside of them, MyLinda and Michael in one box, and David and Gene in the other. They were rolling them around the yard and bumping into each other, and having a great time!

Our parents were products of the great depression. Where there was little to give. They were now living in a time of plenty, and they wanted their grandchildren to have what they had only dreamt about themselves, and what they had always wanted to give to their own children. Grandparents in their great zeal to show how much they love their grandchildren sometimes give them everything they want or can think of.

With the hundreds of dollars spent by parents and grandparents for Christmas, the toys they found of greatest worth were two empty cardboard boxes that didn't cost a dime. There has to be a great lesson in there somewhere. Besides, none of the grandparents were about to be outdone by the other,. Why their grandchildren would never sit and count who gave which gifts, how many, or what. Right?

Christmas Card Boxes
Recycled Project/Gift Wrap

MATERIALS LIST:

last years' Christmas cards
glue
pencil
butter knife or orange stik
scissors
ruler

INSTRUCTIONS:

1.   Pick out a Christmas card that has a design that is fairly centered. Cut it apart at the fold.

2.   Take inside of card (the part with the greeting on it) and cut off a tiny amount (about 1/16", not more than 1/8") off two sides (one short side, and one long side), this will become the bottom of the box.

3.   Turn over card front (box top). Now with a pencil draw a line one inch from the card edge (this will make a one inch deep box). Do this on all four sides.

4.   Repeat the process on the card section with the greeting, but draw the lines on the same side as the greeting. This will put the words on the inside of your box.

5.   Now line up your ruler on each line and use a butter knife or orange stik to score each line (that means press down hard on the line to make an impression). Do this to both halves of the card.

6.   Now with your scissors cut to where the lines intersect on both sides of the short edge.

7.   Fold on the lines, toward the center of box.

8.   Put glue on one of the short edges (the box ends). Fold up the long

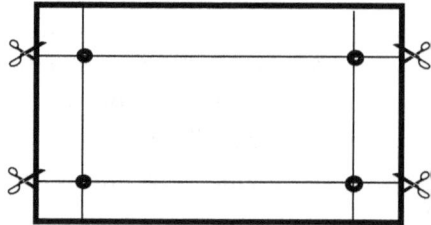

edge, folding in the extensions. Glue extension to inside of short edge. Do one end of the box at a time. Repeat process on the other end. If you are in a hurry use double-stick tape instead.

9. Repeat instruction number 8 for bottom of box.

10. Now place top of box over bottom.

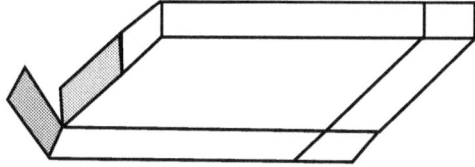

TIP 1: *Score before folding*: Scoring before folding gives a much cleaner, sharper fold and makes the folding easier.

TIP 2: You must make sure that you do not cut more than 1/8 inch off the two edges of greeting section of the card or your bottom will fit too loosely.

VARIATION 1: If you want to change the depth of the box, simply change the amount you measure (i.e. change 1 inch to 1 1/2 inch or 3/4 inch, etc.).

VARIATION 2: For a little more fun skip the gluing and fold each edge in half (mark and score before folding). Then fold the extensions in on both sides of one end and fold the short end over both extensions. You now have a folded box with no glue and have decreased the depth of the box by half.

VARIATION 3: You don't have to use old Christmas cards. If you want to create your own boxes simple cut out two identical pieces of index weight paper and color your own design on one side. Then follow the directions above.

VARIATION 4: Buy a piece of poster board and make a really big box. Just determine how deep you need your box, then mark, score and fold according to the directions above.

Once you get started you won't want to stop!

Mom's Pumpkin Pie

1	large can of pumpkin
3	cups sugar
1	cup flour
1	teaspoon salt
1	teaspoon cinnamon
1	teaspoon allspice
½	teaspoon nutmeg
½	teaspoon ginger
2	cans evaporated milk (or 3¼ cup milk)
4	eggs

Preheat oven to 350° F. Place pumpkin, sugar, flour, salt and spices together in a large bowl, mix until smooth. Now add eggs and milk and mix until a creamy consistency. Pour into prepared pie shells and bake for 45-55 minutes. A knife inserted into center of pie should come out clean when pie is done.

Makes 5 regular or 3 deep dish pies

VARIATION: 1 When I was growing up my Grandma Va loved pecans and put them in almost everything, but this pie has always been one of my favorite pies. Grandma called it Pepunk Pie, and she used to either cover the top of each pie with chopped pecans or take the pecan halves and make decorations on the top of each. Either way Pepunk (pecan and pumpkin) Pie is worth trying on at least on of these pies.

VARIATION: 2 Just as I loved eating Pepunk Pie my father loved Pumpkin Custard. Mom used to make three pies and then add an extra egg and about 1/2 cup more milk to remaining batter. She would pour it into a greased glass bowl and set that bowl into a pan of water and bake it with the rest of the pumpkin pies. Sometimes she would bake them in small custard cups and serve them with a dollop of whipped cream on top. Very Tasty!

Yes I Can

MyLinda Butterworth

ONCE there was a train name Clara; she was a bright shiny blue engine and today she was pulling several cars filled with Christmas toys for the children who lived way over on the other side of the mountain. As she went speeding on her way across the country to deliver her goods; her wheels went around very fast, squealing along on the track. Choo, choo! Chug-a-Chug! Choo, choo! Chug-a-Chug! She was very happy. Only once a year did she get the privilege of carrying toys just for Christmas, and Clara was in a hurry today to deliver her goods on time.

But, all of a sudden, BANG! Right at the foot of the mountain Clara broke down! Chug-a-Chug! Chug! Chug! Squeak! Choooo! The wheels slid along the track and then came to a complete stop. She couldn't go any farther. How in the world could she ever get across the mountains now in time for the children's Christmas?

Rag dolls, clown dolls, toy soldiers, little toy wagons and carts, doll houses, Noah's arks, bats and balls and so much more—were all stuck at the bottom of the mountain. Clara felt very sad as she stood there hoping that someone would come along to help her. Then suddenly, "toot, toot, toot!" Along came a Great Strong Red Engine, all finely cleaned up and shining with his number plate scoured and bright. He had just finished his work of pulling a fine long passenger train, with sleeping cars and a dining-car to the big city. That was a fine thing to do and he was puffing with pride.

"O Big, Big Engine?" cried the Train while her cars all joined in the chorus. "Will you please take us over the mountain? Our Engine has broken down, and we're loaded with Christmas toys for the children on the other side. Will you help us, help us, please?"

But the Great Big Red Passenger Engine blew off stream with a shrieeeeek. He puffed himself up with pride to make himself look very big and important. "It's not my businesssss," he roared, "to pull such a little nobody as you! I pull only fine passenger cars. I can't be bothered with the likes of you! Puff, puff! Ding, Dong! Wheu-eu-shhhh!"

And with that he switched himself round on a sidetrack, passed the poor little train and soon left her helpless and far behind. Well, the little Train and its' cars felt sad but she never stopped hoping that someone would come along and help her.

Then before Clara had time to dry her tears along came a Great Big Black Freight Engine. He had just pulled a freight train over the mountain and was on his way back to the roundhouse to take a nap. Quickly Clara and her cars called to the Freight Engine: "O Big, Big Engine will you please take us over the mountain? Our Engine has broken down, and we're loaded with Christmas toys for the children on the other side. Will you help us, help us, please?"

But the Big Black Freight Engine snorted. He snorted and snorted and puffed, sending up out of his smokestack a shower of angry sparks. "I've done enough work for today! Yes-s-s-s Ss-s-s-sir-ee!" he hissed. "I'm off for a little res-s-st! I've done enough, done enough!"

Then he switched himself round on to the sidetrack and passed the poor little train and her cars, and soon left her far behind! Clara now felt very, very, very sad; but she never stopped hoping that someone would come to help her.

Time passed and soon down the tracks came a Rusty, Dusty, Dingy Brown Engine slowly dragging along the rails, he was just about the same size as Clara. This tired old Engine was sighing and moaning and grunting. He was rumbling and grumbling and groaning. But still the little train and all her cars called out: "O Engine, Engine will you please take us over the mountain? Our Engine has broken down, and we're loaded with Christmas toys for the children on the other side. Will you help us, help us, please?"

Then the Rusty, Dusty, Dingy Brown Engine groaned and grunted and grumbled: " I never could pull you! I couldn't! I haven't the strength! No, No! I never could, I never, never could!" And with that he dragged himself round on the sidetrack, passed the poor little train and her cars and soon left her far behind. Poor little Clara was sad, but she never stopped hoping that someone would some to help them.

So after a very long time, along came a Small Little Yellow Engine, an engine so very small it seemed useless to ask for help; yet he had one bright, lively eye shining out in his head, and he was humming and hurrying, whistling and ringing his bell in the very liveliest way.

So the little Train cried out, while her Cars all joined in the chorus: "O Little Engine? will you please take us over the mountain? Our Engine has broken down, and we're loaded with Christmas toys for the children on the other side. Will you help us, help us, please?"

Now the Small Little Yellow Engine had never been far away from the freight yard; he had spent all his days in the switching yard. But think of all those children without their Christmas toys! He couldn't let the train stand still and the children have no toys for Christmas, so he started to chug up steam and she answered; "Yes, I'm sure I can!"

Then he came straight up to Clara and her shiny blue train and said, "My name is Timmy and ...," he then took a big gulp, smiled and said, "I'm sure I can pull you over the mountain." Then Timmy the Small Little Yellow Engine caught hold and started to pull! He tugged and he tugged and he pulled! Pretty soon, Ding, Dong! Ding, Dong! Puff, puff! Chug, chug! The train-of-cars began to move! Slowly, oh so slowly the train began to move! The Small Little Yellow Engine kept tugging and pulling. And as he tugged he kept tugging, slowly, very slowly: "Yes—Yes—Yes—I—can! Yes—Yes—Yes—I—can!"

Steadily Timmy gained speed and as he did he puffed out faster: "Yes—I—can! Yes—I—can! Yes—I—can!"

Slow and steady up the track Timmy climbed. Clara, her cars and all the toys were cheering on Timmy saying, "Yes—you—can! Yes—you—can!" That made Timmy work harder and he puffed very fast: "Yes—I—can! Yes—I—can! Yes—I—can!"

At last, just as the Small Little Yellow Engine was about to run out of steam he reached the top of the mountain! He was on top of the world! He'd climbed that big, long slope! He'd done it! He had really done it! He looked down the other side of the mountain and saw the town below and thought of all the happy children waiting for the train load of toys and smiled. Then Timmy gave one long puff of smoke, "I knew I could! I knew I could! I knew I could!" he puffed.

Then down the hill he barreled, going faster and faster and feeling stronger and stronger. And as he puffed along he kept singing, "I knew I could! I knew I could! I knew I could! I knew I could! I knew I could!"

As Clara the bright blue engine and her train of cars pulled slowly into the station her wheels squealed with delight. But Timmy, the Small Little Yellow engine was happier still and let out a big sigh of contentment, Whooooosh!. The toys were delivered on time for Christmas and Timmy had accepted the challenge to climb the mountain and had won. "I KNEW I COULD!" he said and headed to the round house for a well deserved rest.

Christmas Train
Art Project/Decoration

MATERIALS LIST:

3 apple boxes, tops and bottoms   *gift wrapping paper*
white glue   *2 sheets black poster board*
scissors   *pliers*
utility knife   *masking tape*
empty plastic 3 gallon ice cream bucket
2 pieces red construction paper   *wire*
pencil   *ruler*

assorted decorations (fringe, garlands, jingle bells, dolls, teddy bear, etc.)

INSTRUCTIONS:

1. Separate boxes. Set bottom boxes aside for train cars.

2. To make base of engine use 1 apple box top. Cover outside of box with wrapping paper and set aside.

3. To make cab of engine use other apple box top. Place box on end and cut three 4 x 6 inch windows, four inches from top of standing box. Cover with wrapping paper and secure edges with white glue. Cover inside of later box if desired.

4. Place ice cream carton lid on front of cab below front window at the bottom of box. Pierce two holes through lid and box. Thread a piece of wire through lid and box and back through box and lid twist tight on front of box.

5. Take engine base that you covered in step 2 and place cab box on top of base at one end lining up box edges. Pierce four holes through

base and cab. Wire boxes together. Twisting wires together with pliers underneath base, then cover wires with masking tape for additional security and stability.

6. Take two pieces of red construction paper and measure the depth of your ice cream carton, cut accordingly. Attach construction paper around the outside of ice cream carton. Cut a circle the size of the bottom of the carton out of wrapping paper and attach with circles of tape to end of carton. Now put the ice cream carton back on the lid to finish the engine.

7. For the box cars. Cover the apple box bottoms with wrapping paper, gluing edges down to secure. You can cover inside if you wish.

8. To make caboose (which my daughter said we could not forget): cover the outside of an apple box bottom as directed in 7, then turn it upside down. Cut out several windows and glue them in the appropriate place. You could also wrap a matching shoe box and glue it on top to make the look complete.

9. To make the wheels, use black poster board: for large engine wheels use a dinner plate to trace around, make 2. For smaller wheels use saucers to trace around, 4 for engine and 4 for each box car. Cut out all the wheels and glue them in the appropriate places on the boxes.

10. At this point additional decorations may be added. Fringe around windows, cow catcher on front, garlands around box cars, smoke stack on top of engine with stuffing coming out of it to represent smoke, headlights as eyes, pom pom for nose, big smile for lips, Teddy Bears and Dolls seating on box inside cab waving through windows, etc. These are all optional ideas. Name for train could be Butterworth (your family name) Express.

11. Place train with cars around base of tree. There should be one box car for each child. You can put their name on the outside of the car and then wait for Santa to fill it or place gifts for that child in their box as they arrive. Then use the box on Christmas day to collect all the wrapping paper.

Gumdrop Cake

1½	lb mixed gumdrops diced
1	box seedless dates diced
2	cups chopped nuts
1	cup butter
2	cups sugar
3	cups flour
4	eggs
½	cup buttermilk
1	teaspoon vanilla

Preheat oven to 300° F. Mix together gumdrops (flat ones are best, cut into quarters), dates and nuts with one cup of flour. Cream together butter and sugar. Beat in 4 eggs. Add rest of flour, buttermilk and vanilla to mixture. Fold in the gum drop mixture. Bake for approximately 2 hours in greased tube pan until toothpick comes out clean.

Makes 12-18 servings

NOTE: This is a great replacement for those who don't like fruitcake. Just for fun try using spiced gumdrops instead of fruit flavored ones.

GIFT SUGGESTION: Place on an inexpensive serving plate and fill the center of the cake with leftover gumdrops.

The Bear Who Couldn't Sleep
[On Christmas Eve]
Robert O. Day

Cast: Narrator   Barnibus Blakely Bartholomew Bear
         Beavie Beaver   Freddie Frog
         Sneaky Snake   Redheaded Woodpecker
         Who the Owl   Ghost
         Witch   Sandman

NARRATOR: [Enters and crosses while talking with audience to cave entrance.] Once upon a time, a long, long time ago out in the middle of the great woods there lived a bear. Now, he was a great big bear, with great big paws, a great big body, a great big head, and the ability to speak, or growl or snore so loudly that everyone in the forest could hear him. That's the reason that he lived in the cave in the side of the great mountain, because that's the only place that he could go each night to sleep that his snoring wouldn't keep everyone else in the forest awake.

BEAR: [Laying down with back to audience.] Awhhh, their just jealous that they can't snore as well as I can. It doesn't bother me any to snore, I just sleep right through it.

NARRATOR: Yes, so we've noticed in the past. Well, as I was saying, this great big bear's fur coat was a reddish-brown in color........

BEAR: [Sits up and turns around to face audience.] And isn't it beautiful? I rub it up against a big old tree just down the trail there every day to keep it shiny and bright.....Not only that, [demonstrates] uhh....it feels good to scratch my back and....

NARRATOR: As I was saying, this great bear's fur was a reddish- brown. [Bear reacts to narration.] His eyes were large and friendly, and he was just a very nice person to know. Nice, that is, as long as he got enough sleep every night. But when he didn't get enough sleep, he became a very grouchy bear that growled and snapped at everyone. When ever that happened, no one even wanted to be in the same forest with him. By the way, did I mention yet what his name is? I haven't? Please excuse the oversight, his name is Barnibus Blakely Bartholomew Bear......

BEAR: Huh? You called?

NARRATOR: No, I was just telling the boys and girls what your name is.

BEAR: Oh! Well, that's O.K., but tell them what my friends call me.

NARRATOR: Alright, his friends call him Barney.

BEAR: That's right, Barnibus Blakely Bartholomew Bear. Great buzzing bees, why do you want them to know my whole name for!? Great buzzing bees! [Starts yawning and stretching.] I sure should be getting sleepy.....But I'm not! Grrrrr, I'm not!

NARRATOR: Sure enough. It is time that Barney should be going to sleep, otherwise Santa won't be able to come and it won't be Christmas, but he surely isn't sleepy.....[Aside] What he is, is grouchy! I wonder where the Sandman is? He has never been late like this before, especially not on Christmas Eve.

BEAR: Well, he's late this time. [Stands up and move toward Narrator.] And who said I was getting grouchy? Who said? You trying to get me in trouble with Santa, Great buzzing bees. [Go on grumbling and mumbling under the narrator.]

NARRATOR: I certainly hope that the Sandman hurries. Out in the forest, all the creatures who live there, who should also be asleep by now are all still awake as well. [Various animal sounds are heard.] Night time has come to the woods. The sun has just slipped behind the last hill, and all of the stars in the heavens are beginning to twinkle just as they do every night. Even the moon has come up on time, but everyone in the forest is still awake.

BEAR: What's all that blasted noise out there? How's a bear to sleep with all that racket going on? [Cross to cave opening] I'll fix them, I'll just tell everyone in the forest to **be quiet!**

NARRATOR: And that's just what he did too. He walked right over to the opening in his cave, put his great big bear head outside, and growled......

BEAR: [Yells] **KNOCK OFF THE NOISE, I'M TRYING TO SLEEP IN HERE!** [Animal sounds stop.]......Well that sure quieted them down! [Turns and starts back to bed.]

NARRATOR: And it did... [Pause a few seconds and listen.] ...for about 10 seconds. Then Barney heard a chewing sound. No, it was more like a chomp or a crunch. [Barney reacts to narration.] Well, what ever it was it made Barney mad because it was still a noise. [Narrator follows Bear.] So he walked right out of his cave, and right down the path toward the river where the noise was coming from. The closer he got to the river the louder the chewing sound became.....

BEAVER: **TIMBERRRRRRRRRRRR!!!!!!** [Tree falls in front of Barney, almost hitting him.] What's the matter with you Barney? Didn't you hear my TIMBERRRRR!!!!? What are you trying to do, get bumped on the head? It's getting so's a beaver can't get anything done around here without having to worry about hitting great big reddish-brown bears on the head. Why don't you watch where you're going? Didn't you see my sign?

BEAR: Sign? What sign?

BEAVER: That one right over there on the tree. It distin<u>ct</u>ly says, "Caution, beavers at work. Dam being constructed, please detour." Can't you read?

BEAR: Sure I can read, but not in the dark. Beavers aren't supposed to work after dark anyway, everybody knows that... Especially on Christmas eve. Santa will never come with all that racket!

BEAVER: [Mockingly] "Beavers aren't supposed to work after dark anyway, everyone knows that," **BIRCHBARK!** Beavers always work until they begin to get sleepy. I'm not sleepy yet, and so I am still at work, so go away and let me get back to my dam building. Shooo, shooo, shooooo.

BEAR: Say Beavie, you're right! You do always work until you start getting sleepy, but you usually start getting sleepy about the time it starts to get dark. But the moon is already out and so are the stars, so it's dark already.......why aren't you asleep?

BEAVER: Because I'm not sleepy, now will you please go away and let me get back to work? Old budinsky bear, everyone knows that beavers have to stay busy, busy, busy, except when we're asleep.

BEAR: But Beavie, why aren't you sleepy yet? Why aren't I not sleepy yet? What time is it?

NARRATOR: While the two of them were busy trying to figure out why sleep had not yet come to the forest, a little green frog jumped up on a lily pad at the waters edge and began to sing....

FROG: Oh...It's ....night outside and time to sing. Oh....It's ....night outside and time to sing. Singing on a pad's not bad, but being a frog I prefer a log. [Frog jumps off lily pad and onto tree beaver cut down.] High ya guys, high ya, high ya, Needeep!

BEAVER That's all I need, another interruption. I'll never get back to work at this rate.

FROG: What are you fellas doing up at this time of night? I've been watching for Santa, but I never saw you up around here at night before. Why aren't you in bed asleep? [Reaches out and catches a fly.]

BEAR: Because I'm not sleepy that's why! You wanta make something out of it? GRRRR!

NARRATOR: [Snake starts to quietly enter.] Just then, slithering up out of a hole next to a pile of rocks by the side of the path came a snake. He was a very pretty snake with bright red, blue and Green circles around his body. Out of his mouth, at a very high rate of speed, flicked a little pink forked tongue. Do you see it?

SNAKE: [Using breathy delivery] SSSSSSSSay fellas and girlssss, what'ssss going on here [Frog sees snake and jumps onto Bear's shoulders, leaning over his head.] on the forest path in the early hours of the night? SSSSure is hard to get to ssssleep with all thissss noissss going on sssssssssss.

FROG: Yipes! What is that? **<u>NEEDEEP!</u>**

BEAR: Will you get off of my head?!? Get off of there! [Tries to pull Frog off, but he won't let go.]

BEAVER: It's only Sneaky Snake Freddie Frog. For goodness sake, he won't hurt you.

SNAKE: He sssure frightensssss easssily doesssn't he?

BEAR: Get off of my head!

FROG: Not me! Not me! I'm staying right here until that monster goes away!

BEAR: [Throws hands in the air.] I wish I was in my cave asleep!

BEAVER: So do I! Then maybe I could still get some work done.

SNAKE: Ssssay, why aren't you assssleep, Barney my friend? Sssss.

BEAR: Because I'm just **not sleepy!**

FROG: No, but you sure are getting grouchy!

BEAR: I am not! Get off of my head you dumb frog!

FROG: No way! No way! Not until Sneaky Snake is gone. Needeep! Needeep!

NARRATOR: [Woodpecking sounds begin] About that time, way up in the top of a tree a Redheaded Woodpecker began to peck at a tree.

BEAR: [Looking up] Oh no! Now what? [Shouting] Hey you! Up in that tree! **Knock-it-off**! How can anyone get any sleep with all that racket going on!?

NARRATOR: For a moment the noise stopped and just as Barney began to smile because it was quiet, down from the top of the tree flew the woodpecker, red head and all. [Lands on tree across the path beside the snake and begins to peck a hole in the tree.]

SNAKE: [Leaning back on knees and revolving in a circle, hands clutched to chest.] Heaven ssssave me, I've been sssshot! Sssss.

BEAVER: No you haven't been shot, that's only a woodpecker.

SNAKE: Then I've been **Woodpecked! Ssssave me!**

FROG: No you haven't been woodpecked. Open your eyes and look beside you, it's only a redheaded woodpecker.

WOODPECKER: [Indignantly] What do you mean, **only** a redheaded woodppppecker? I'm the only redheaded woodppppecker in this wood, and I'm very fond of pppparties. What kind of a pppparty do you have going on here, a Christmas ppppparty?

BEAR: This is not a party, I'm trying to get everyone to go home and go to sleep so I can!

WOODPECKER: [Excited] It isn't a pppparty? That's ppppretty bad to have so many pppppeople ppppppresent on Christmas eve and not have a pppparty....[Looks at each one and shakes head as they do.]

FROG: [Shakes head, no] It's not a party.

BEAVER: [Shakes head, no] No party!

SNAKE: Sssssorry, no party.

WOODPECKER: [Sadly] No ppparty......[thinking]...Let's pppplan a ppparty then!

BEAVER: [Irritated] No, we're not having a party, will you please get out of my construction site and let me get back to work! Great pinebark!

BEAR: Hey, what are you doing up in the middle of the night? Birds all go to sleep at night, so why aren't you asleep?

WOODPECKER: For the same reason you're not asleeppp, we're having a ppparty!

EVERYONE: No, we're **not** having a pppparty!

WOODPECKER: Oh, that's too bad, but it was a good idea while it lasted. But you know of course that you're wrong. There are some birds that don't sleeppp at night. They sleeppp during the daytime and stay awake all night.

BEAR: Oh yea! Who?

WOODPECKER: That's right.

FROG: What's right?

WOODPECKER: Bear's right.

BEAR: I'm right? What did I say?

FROG: Yes, what did he say?

BEAR: Frog, will you **please** get of my head? [Pulls at Frog.]

FROG: Not with that Sneaky Snake down there.

BEAR: Oh brother! Now woodpecker, I'm getting very **cross**! **Who** stays awake all night?

WOODPECKER: That's right! Who is one of those that stays awake all night.

BEAVER: Who?

WOODPECKER: Who the owl. Everybody knows Who the owl. He's the wisest bird in the whole forest. He's pppretty smart.

BEAR: Where does he live? If he's so darn smart, maybe he can solve this riddle of why no one is asleep on Christmas eve.

WOODPECKER: Who lives in a great big tree just down the ppppath, here let me draw you a mapppp.....[Woodpecker moves over and starts to draw on ground with his beak, others gather around.]

NARRATOR: [Characters mime narrator's description.] Well, the redheaded woodpecker told everyone where the owl lived and how to get there. And, after some discussion, it was decided that Barney being the biggest and bravest of the creatures would go through the woods to talk to the owl. And so he did.[Bear starts walking others move to assigned spots.] He walked through the dark woods where the branches of the trees hung over the path like long arms reaching out to grab him. [Jumps] But he wasn't afraid, he was just grouchy because he was having to go without his sleep. Finally he arrived at the owl's house.

BEAR: HEY, YOU UP THERE IN THE TREE! HEY OWL, ARE YOU HOME? Great buzzing bees!

OWL: [Sticking his head out.] **Whooo** is the name, whoooo are you, and what do yoooou want?

BEAR: I'm Barney Bear and I've been told that you are pretty smart, is that right?

OWL: Wrong! I am not smart, I am **wise**. There's a difference, you know.

BEAR: [Amazed, scratching head] Is that so? I didn't know that, you **are** pretty smart....

OWL: No, wise!

BEAR: Oh......Then can you tell me Who, why is it that no one in the forest is asleep tonight? Why can't I go to sleep?

OWL: Elementary, my dear bear. It is because the Sandman has not been through the forest yet. He will not be coming tonight or any other night.

BEAR: He won't, why not?

OWL: Because the ugly old witch who lives in the middle of the forest has captured him and put him into a cage in her house.

BEAR: Why would she do a dumb thing like that? Doesn't she know that everyone needs to sleep.

OWL: She doesn't like to sleep, besides she hates Christmas and doesn't want Santa to come.

BEAR: Hates Christmas, how can **anyone** hate Christmas. Why everyone has been good **alllll** year long so that Santa can come on Christmas eve and bring lots of goodies....

OWL: But she likes to stay up all night and be very mean and grouchy. And because she is so mean, she never gets anything on Christmas but a lump of coal. She want's everyone to be grumpy so they will get a lump of coal too.

BEAR: Oh she does, does she? Well, we'll see about that.

NARRATOR: [Characters again mime narration.] Barney was so angry that he decided to go to the witch's house and make the old witch let the sandman go. After getting directions to the witch's house he started out running through the forest. He stumbled over roots and vines and things in the dark, but he didn't care. It just made him all the madder. Finally he came to a clearing in the middle of the woods where the witch's house stood. An eerie looking white thing came floating out of the witch's chimney and headed straight for Barney.

GHOST: OOOOOOOOOOH, go back you bear or you'll loose your reddish-brown hairrrr, OOOOOOOOOOOOh, go back before the witch geeeeets youuuuuu.

BEAR: Get out of my way or I'll turn you into a bed sheet and sleep on you GRRRRR!

GHOST: [Running away] OOOOOOOOOOOH NOOOOOOOOOOOOOOOOOOO!

NARRATOR: Barney was so grouchy that he even frightened the ghost. But Barney had made so much noise growling at the ghost that inside of the house the witch heard him and quickly locked the door. [Barney bangs on the door.]

WITCH: Whose there?

BEAR: It's me, Barnibus Blakely Bartholomew Bear, and I want to come in!

146

WITCH: Go away Barney Bear, you can't come in here!

BEAR: Don't you call me Barney Bear, you're no friend of mine. I know you have the Sandman locked up in there. You're keeping me from my sleep and Santa from coming to the forest. Now you let me in! GRRRRRRR!

WITCH: [Dancing back and forth as she speaks.] Growl if you wish, I don't care, you won't get in here you silly old bear! Hey, that's pretty good, I made it rhyme that time, [Cackles] HEHEHEHEHEHE!

BEAR: That did it, by bees wax! [Backs up, runs, and leaps into the air hitting the door and smashing it to the ground.]

WITCH: [Screaming] AAAAHHHHHH! You get out of here you old bear, before I turn you into a toad!

BEAR: If you don't let the Sandman out of that cage, I'm going to bite you right on the end of your long warty nose. GRRRR! [Bear chases witch around room and finally goes by cage.]

NARRATOR: The Sandman knew that the old witch could turn Barney into a toad if she got the chance, and he didn't want that to happen. He knew the only reason that Barney was so grouchy was that he had lost too much sleep. So, quick as a flash he reached out through the bars of the cage and grabbed his bag of magic sand off of the table and threw some into Barney's eyes and ....[Bear suddenly stops, falls on floor with feet in the air and begins to snore loudly.]

BEAR: [Snoring very loudly] ZZZZZZZZZZZZZZZZ!

WITCH: [Covering ears with hands.] What is that terrible noise? Oh, that's terrible, I can't stand that noise! What is it? Make it stop! [Screams] **Make it stop!**

BEAR: [Stops snoring and sits straight up.] Huh, what, who, when... Who woke me up just when I was starting to sleep? GRRRR, that **really** makes me mad!

WITCH: I did you dumb bear! Your snoring was driving me crazy. I'll fix you, I'll turn you into a toad before you can get back to sleep. And as for you Mr. Sandman, give me that sleep making sand or I'll turn you into a toad too. [Cackles] HEHEHEHEHEHEHEHE!

[Witch moves toward Sandman, but is countered by Barney trying to bite her on the nose.]

BEAR: GRRRRR, I'm going to bite you, you old witch, right on your ugly nose!

WITCH: What? Oh no! HELP, leave me alone, get away you old bear. I'll zap you! [Sandman grabs large handful of sand and throws it on Barney who falls to sleep at once with all feet in the air.]

BEAR: [Louder than before, continue under following dialogue.] **ZZZZZZZZZZZZZZZ!**

WITCH: Oh no! Not that again! Please not that again! I can't stand that snoring, please make it stop. I'll do anything, please, **please** make it **stop**!

SANDMAN: You'll do anything?

WITCH: Yes...anything, only, **please** make him **stop**!

SANDMAN: First, you have to let me out of the cage, and promise to let us go and never bother us again, ever.

WITCH: I promise, witches honor [crosses eyes and arms and waves hands up and down.], anything, just make him stop!

[Witch lets Sandman out of cage, he crosses to Bear pulls a large brightly colored hanky from his pocket and wipes some of the sand from Barney's eyes. Then he shakes him gently until he sits up.]

SANDMAN: Now you old witch, I'll take Barney back to his cave and leave you alone. From now on I'll never come to visit you again and you can just stay awake all the time.

NARRATOR: [Characters react appropriately to the narration.] And with that the Sandman took Barney and they left the old witch standing in the middle of her house with her hands over her ears because she was afraid Barney might go back to sleep again. [Witch finally turns and walks away.] From that time until this the Sandman has never gone back to visit the witch, which of course is why witches stay up all night, never go to sleep and are usually so grouchy.

BEAR: I hope there's still time to get home and go to sleep so Santa will come. I'm really worried.

SANDMAN: [Stops and pulls a large watch from his pocket and looks at it.] Let's see what time it is......Hummmm, it is almost morning.

BEAR: Oh no, I guess we won't have any Christmas in the forest this year because everyone is still awake.

SANDMAN: Well, there **is** one way to turn the clock back.

BEAR: How, how, tell me, please tell me.

SANDMAN: It takes a good deed, someone who will give up something that belongs to them. But it has to be given in the next minute or it's too late.

BEAR: **I'll** do it, I'll **do** it, but what, what?

SANDMAN: It has to be something really valuable to you Barney, hurry, hurry!

BEAR: If only I were asleep, when I'm asleep I dream up great things.... I fall asleep, then I snore and dream and snore and dream....

SANDMAN: That's it Barney, share your dreams....

BEAR: But I can't dream until I start to snore.

SANDMAN: Then that's what you need to give up, your snoring so everyone can share your dreams.

BEAR: You mean I wouldn't be able to snore and dream anymore?

SANDMAN: No Barney, you only have to share. Hurry, make up your mind we're about out of time.

BEAR: O.K., I'll do it. GREAT BUZZING BEES, I'LL DO IT!

SANDMAN: Alright Barney, here we go. [Reaches into bag and hits him with a bit handful of sleep sand. Barney falls backward and immediately goes to sleep.]

BEAR: [Snoring loudly.] **ZZZZZZZZZZZZZZZ!**

SANDMAN: [Takes a bag out and holds it to Bear's mouth to collect the Z's. Then he fills another bag and another. Barney is now snoring softly.] There, that should do it. I have enough Z's in here to put all of the creatures in the forest to sleep. Now, I'll turn this clock back and get to work. Come on Barney, wake up and give me a hand.

BEAR: [Slowly sits up rubbing his eyes.] Huhhh? Is it Christmas yet? Has Santa come?

SANDMAN: Not yet Barney, but the clock has been turned back an hour. That's just enough time to get everyone to sleep so Santa **can** come. Come on, give me a hand. You'll have to carry these two bags of Z's, they are too heavy for me.

BEAR: [Gets up and takes a bag in each hand, following Sandman.] O.K. I'm coming.

NARRATOR: Well, Barney and the Sandman made their rounds through the forest and put every creature to sleep, except Who, because Owls don't sleep at night.

SANDMAN: [Takes little bag from big one and sprinkles it over characters one at a time.] Goodnight Redheaded Woodpecker. Sorry you had to be up so late.

WOODPECKER: That's O.K., [Yawning] I almost got to go to a ppparty. Good [Yawn] night. ZZZZZZZZZ!

SANDMAN: Goodnight Sneaky Snake, go back to your hole and have pleasant dreams.

SNAKE: Goodnight [Yawn] Sssssssandman. Sssssee you [Yawn] tomorrow.

SANDMAN: Goodnight Freddie Frog. Jump off your lily pad and go to bed.

FROG: O.K., goodnight. Good [Yawn] night. Needeep! Needeep to sleep. ZZZZZZZZZ!

SANDMAN: Goodnight Beavie Beaver. It's way past time to stop your work for the night. I'm sorry I'm so late, but have pleasant dreams.

BEAVER: Goodnight. I don't [Yawn] mind that you were late. I [Yawn] sure got a lot of extra work done, [Yawn] once I got rid of that big bear. ZZZZZZZZZZZZZZ!

NARRATOR: One by one all of the creatures had been put to sleep, all except Barney. He had walked through the forest with the sandman dragging those two bags which were now just about empty. But now they had finally come to his cave.

SANDMAN: Goodnight Barney. Thank you for rescuing me from the witch. I know how tired you must be from loosing all that sleep, but you're home now and can lay right down and go to sleep.

BEAR: [Lays down and yawns] Good night Mr. Sandman. Before you go, come here and let me tell you something.

SANDMAN: [Crosses to Bear and leans down and lets Bear whisper to him]. O.K. Barney, I understand. I'll take care of it. You go to sleep now so Santa can come. [Sprinkles sand on him.] Thanks Barney, You're a good bear and I love you. [Turns and crosses down to the audience.] Barney wants me to share his gift with you so that on Christmas eve you will be able to go right to sleep too. [Opens bag and rummages around with his head in side, then looks up at audience and counts here and there, then puts head back inside bag.] There are still a lot of Barney's magic left in here, but there's not enough Z's, so I guess It won't work.

NARRATOR: [Moves toward Sandman.] Are you sure there isn't something you can do?

SANDMAN: Well, as a matter of fact, if everyone who takes a little bag of magic put's their **own Z** inside and then sets it aside until Christmas eve, it will work just fine.

NARRATOR: Will all of you be willing to do that? Pick up a little bag of sleep magic and then when you get home write a big Z on a slip of paper and put it in the bag, then put it on the dresser and wait until Christmas eve before you use it? **O.K.** Good. Thanks Sandman!

SANDMAN: Don't thank me, it was Barney's idea. Let's thank him. Thanks Barney, we love you, sleep tight. Give Barney a big **Z** so he can sleep tight! ZZZZZZZZZZZZZZ! Merry Christmas and......

VOICE: [Sleigh bells are heard getting louder and closer.]....**to all a goodnight!**

FINI

Finger Puppets

(to accompany the play "The Bear Who Couldn't Sleep")

Art Project/Family Entertainment

MATERIALS:

> *photocopy of patterns*
> *colored markers*
> *moveable eyes (optional)*
> *glue*
> *scissors*
> *contact paper*
> *feathers for birds*
> *3x5 inch index cards*

INSTRUCTIONS:

1. Photocopy patterns onto index weight paper.

2. Color all the characters. Laminate or cover front with contact paper to protect the puppets and then cut them out carefully.

3. Using index cards, make a finger roll for each character by cutting card in half. You will get two finger rolls.

4. Wrap three inch section around finger loosely so that finger will slide in and out easily. Glue or tape edges together. Glue finger roll to back of puppet character.

5. For a stage go behind a couch, use an expandable curtain rod with curtain on it three feet up the doorway, or turn a card table turned on it's side with a colorful cloth draped over it.

NOTE: Read the story as a play, role play, make additional props for the puppet play: i.e. witches' house, cage for sandman, trees in forest, etc.

Brownie Shortbread

"Could easily become addicted to these" Mal Bowden - Food Taster

1/2   cup butter or margarine, room temperature
1   cup all purpose flour
1/4   cup granulated sugar
1/4   teaspoon salt

BROWNIE LAYER
1/2   cup butter or margarine, room temperature
1/2   cup semi-sweet chocolate chips
2   large eggs
3/4   cup granulated sugar
3   tablespoons all purpose flour
1/2   teaspoon baking powder

Preheat oven to 350° F. Grease an 11x7 inch or 8x8 inch (for thicker brownies) baking pan. In a bowl beat the butter, flour, sugar and salt until mixture holds together and forms a dough. Press over bottom of pan. Bake 20 minutes or until light golden and firm when touched.

BROWNIE LAYER: Heat butter and chocolate in a small saucepan over low heat, stirring often, until melted. Cool 5 minutes. In a medium size bowl, whisk eggs, sugar, flour and baking powder until blended. Whisk in cooled chocolate mixture. Pour over shortbread base. Bake 20 minutes or until top feels firm. Cool in pan before cutting bars.

Makes 24 bars

VARIATION: Add 1/2 cup chopped nuts to shortbread layer.

The Story of "Silent Night"

as told by MyLinda Butterworth

LATE on an afternoon in 1818 just before Christmas, Father Joseph Mohr, the assistant pastor of the church of St. Nicholas in the small town of Oberndorf in Austrian Tyrol, was called to bless a new-born baby. As he walked home that evening through the newly fallen snow he was impressed by the beauty of the quiet starlit night. He thought of the tiny babe that he had just visited. Joseph wondered if the night that Christ was born, was on such a peaceful night as this. When he arrived home he put his feelings into words and wrote a poem entitled, *Stille Nacht* or *Silent Night*.

The day before Christmas Eve as he was going about his duties at the church, he discovered that the mice had eaten the organ bellows. The organ builder lived in Zillertal and it would be impossible for him to get to the church in time to make the necessary repairs. What could be done about the music for the Christmas service? Father Mohr began to think about the poem he had written and showed it to his friend Franz Gruber, the church choirmaster. Franz took the poem and hurried home. Within an hour, he had written a simple tune for a tenor a bass and two guitars.

The combination of the tune and words were enchanting. On Christmas Eve it was performed by Franz, Joseph and two women singers, with Joseph accompanying on his guitar. The congregation sat silently, stunned by the beauty of the music.

After Christmas the organ builder was able to make it to the small church to repair the organ. Franz Gruber played the song on the organ. The organ builder was entranced with it and asked if he could write down the lyrics and music and play the song at his church in Zillertal. After its introduction to the churchgoers in Zillertal by the organ builder, it became a favorite. They called it *The Song from Heaven*.

Gradually the carol made its way to Leipzig where it was heard by the city's Director of Music, who included it in a concert played before the Queen of Saxony. The Queen was delighted with the music and requested that it should be played in the palace on Christmas Eve (1832) so that her children could learn it.

In 1840, *Silent Night* was published in Leipzig but it was called *A Tyrolean Christmas Carol*. Its popularity spread throughout all of Europe. But no one knew who had written the words and music. It was published again as a four-part hymn with the 'author and composer' unknown. It was rumored that it was written by Michael and Joseph Haydn.

The King of Prussia, Frederick Wilhelm IV, heard the song performed by the entire choir of the Imperial Church in Berlin, in 1854. He was so impressed by the music that he immediately declared that the song was to be sung at all Christmas concerts in his country that Christmas. He then ordered his musicians to find out who had composed the beautiful music.

Sometime after this Franz Gruber's son heard about the song and recognized it as his father's composition. It took thirty-six years for the author and composer to be credited for the music. Today, *Silent Night* is considered to be one of the best known and most beloved pieces of Christmas music in existence.

Tin Can Luminaries
Art Activity

MATERIALS LIST:

20 ounce tin can without ridges(Pineapple cans are a good choice)
½ inch wide satin ribbon
tracing paper or copy of design
Gloss white enamel spray paint
spray primer
2 rubber bands
towel
transparent tape
pencil
scissors
votive candle
sand or gravel
newspaper

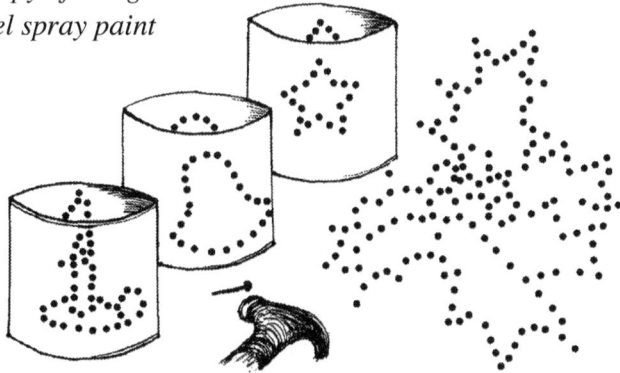

INSTRUCTIONS:

1. Empty the contents from can and remove the label. Clean, then dry the can. Fill the can with water and put it in the freezer. Wait until the water turns to ice.

2. Trace or photocopy the tin punch pattern on the next page. Cut out the pattern along the solid line.

3. Remove the can from the freezer. Wrap the pattern around the can. Fasten the pattern edges together with the tape. Use the rubber bands to hold the pattern in place along the can's edges.

4. Lay a towel down on a hard surface to give you some padding. Place the can on the towel. Use the hammer and nail to punch holes through the dots and into the can. When all the holes are punched, remove the pattern. Let the water melt. Pour out the water and dry the can upside down.

5. Set newspapers out in garage or on porch to paint on. Spray the inside and outside of the can with the paint primer. Let the primer dry. Spray the inside and outside of the can with the white enamel paint. Let the paint dry. Wrap the ribbon around the top of the can and tie a bow. Place sand in the bottom of can, put candle in the sand.

NOTE: These candle holders may be used inside for decoration (make sure you place them on a trivet or pot holder they do get hot) or make several of them and line your sidewalk with them (luminaries). If you use them as luminaries (outside decoration) it is best to put a small amount of sand in the bottom of the can before you put the candle in them. This will keep them from tipping over if a wind comes up as well as providing a safe place for the candle.

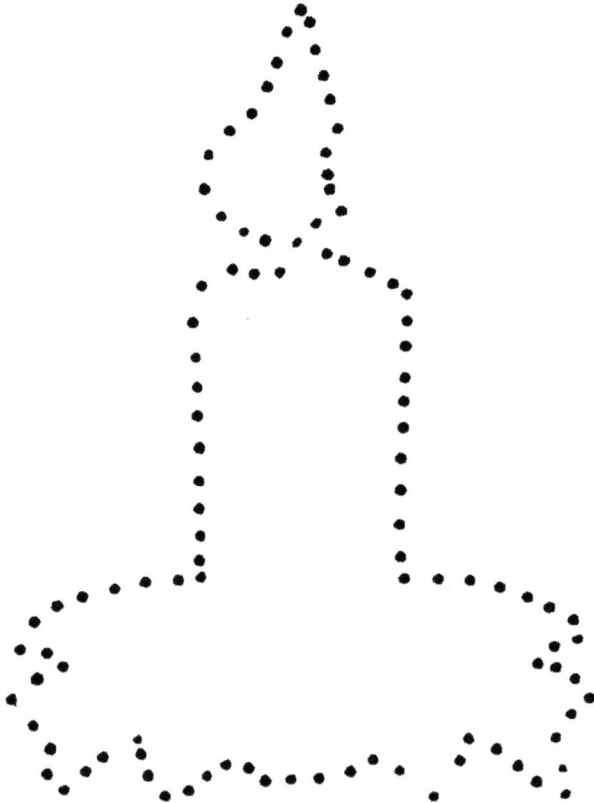

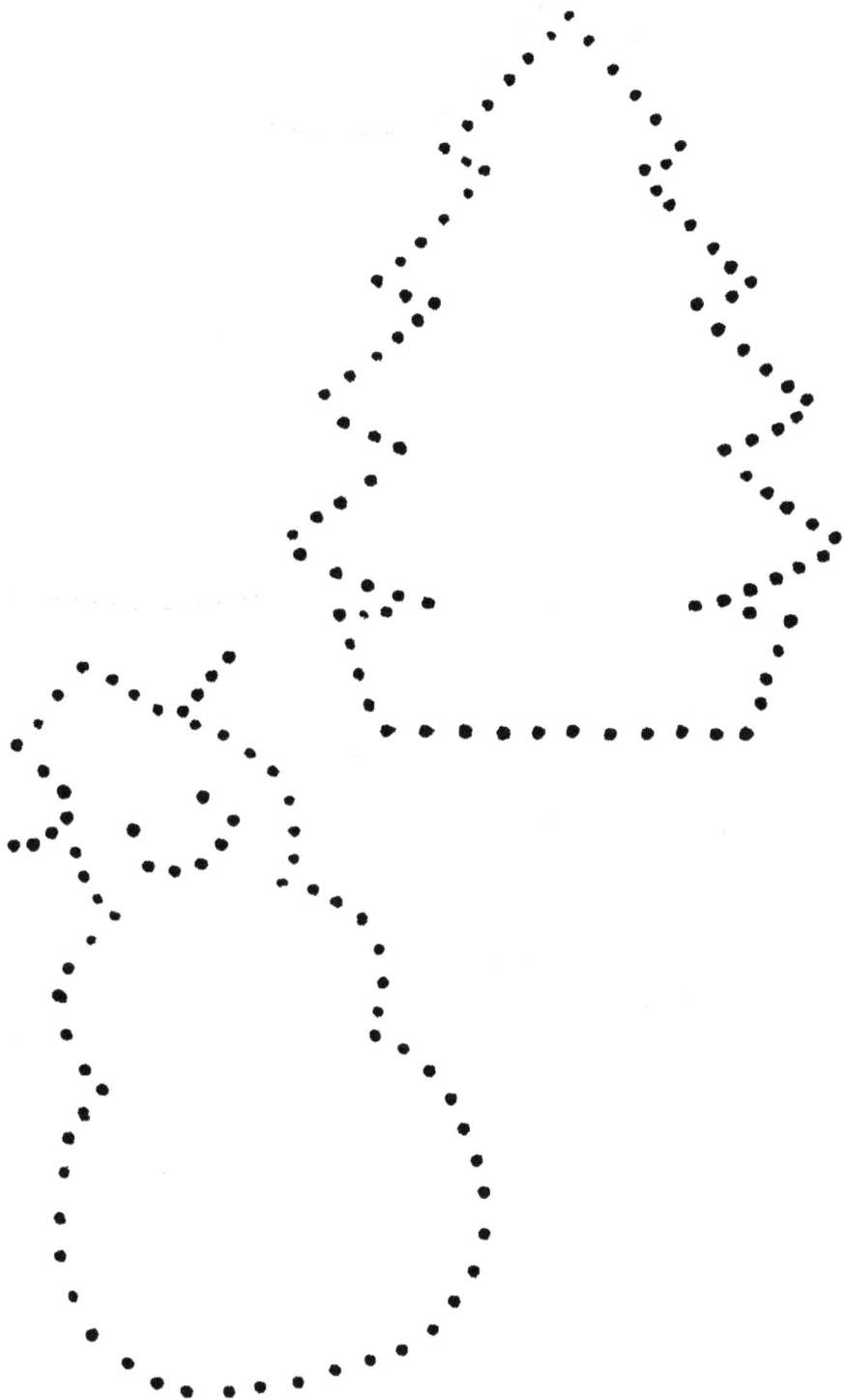

Angel Gingerbread

"A surprisingly mellow taste" Ashley Long - Kitchen Tester

2⅓	cups unbleached flour	1	teaspoon salt
1	teaspoon soda	1	teaspoon ginger
¼	teaspoon cinnamon	¼	teaspoon nutmeg
¼	teaspoon allspice	½	cup brown sugar
½	cup shortening	2	eggs
½	cup molasses	1	cup hot water

Preheat oven to 350° F. Sift dry ingredients into a large mixing bowl. Add shortening, eggs, and molasses. With mixer at medium speed, beat 2 minutes, or beat by hand 300 strokes. Add hot water and mix well. Pour batter into well-greased 13x9x2 inch pan. Bake for 35-40 minutes. Spread Caramel Icing over cake in pan while cake is still warm.

Caramel Icing

¼	cup butter or margarine
1	cup brown sugar
¼	cup cream

Melt butter in sauce pan. Add sugar and cream. Stir over medium heat until sugar is dissolved. Bring to a rolling boil (turn heat back to high), boil 1 minute. Remove from heat and beat immediately. When mixture begins to lose its gloss (about 5 minutes) and starts to thicken, spread quickly over cake in pan, while hot. Cool before cutting.

Hidden Treasures

MyLinda Butterworth

EVERY Christmas we do the same old thing. Put up the tree, send Christmas cards, buy presents, wrap presents, make food, eat food, go to parties ... to say the very least Christmas has lost its glimmer. I mean the advertisers began advertising for Christmas in August this year, so by the time the holiday finally emerges you wish it was over. All my life I was raised to believe that Christmas was a special time of year, a time when all Christians celebrate the birth of the Savior. That is a good thing, but I rarely see or hear anything about that wondrous miracle during the season, except at church. I am surrounded by Santa Claus and his little helpers, advertisements for toys that require batteries which I always seem to forget, signs everywhere which just tell me to buy, spend, put it on credit, or no payments till January. Will someone please tell me where the real reason for the season has gone to?

I guess what really brought all this to light was the night I tried to plug in the Christmas tree lights one evening just a few days before Christmas. I maneuvered my way around the presents under the tree and pushed boxes aside to find the switch to turn on the lights. Earlier in the day a huge package had come from the kids' grandparents in Idaho full of presents, and I had to find a place under the tree for them. As I unloaded the box and began to add them to the already existing mountain of boxes I said to myself, "Where on earth are we going to put all these things when Christmas is over and Santa hasn't even been here yet. There's no room for anymore stuff! These kids have got enough toys now to supply the entire neighborhood with gifts."

I then sat back and looked at our Christmas tree as it twinkled in the early evening light, I saw all the angels hanging on the branches along with the egg carton ornaments made by my children and began to reflect on why we give gifts in the first place. Then it dawned on me that we had let Christmas get totally out of hand and we were going to have to do something to bring it back into perspective. What that was I had no idea, but then I didn't have too much time to think about it. I still needed to make something for the party tonight. I was running so far behind and Christmas was just two days away. I finally got up, but as I turned around I fell over a pile of dolls that were left laying on the floor. As I lay there looking eye to eye with all those dollies, I began to notice the rest of the toys that were strewn from one end of the house to the other. What was I thinking? Whose bright idea was it to have so many toys, half of which they rarely played with. The rest they use as bombs to throw at each other.

Just then my brain kicked in and I remembered the year I spent Christmas with my brother David and his family. That was the year I thought Christmas was going to be a total drag. My husband was 2000 miles away and I was stuck with 4 kids, none of which were mine, and I was expected to be happy. All I could think about was the fact that this Christmas was going to be boring and uneventful, but boy was I wrong. Let me fill you in.

I arrived at my brother's house about 3 or 4 days before Christmas and as usual the place was bustling. I mean, with 4 kids ranging from 2 to 9, I couldn't expect anything else. There was still so much to do, my sister-in-law Vicki still had Christmas shopping to do and presents to wrap. My niece and nephews were constantly sneaking under the tree shaking every present that had their name on it trying to figure out what was in it. The oven I don't think ever got turned off. I felt like I was in a race car heading for the finish line, everything was going by so fast I didn't have time to think about my dilemma.

The day before Christmas, David gathered all the children into the family room and said, "Do you know what day this is?" The room began to echo with answers: "Christmas Eve!' 'Santa comes tonight!' 'I get to open one present!' 'Eat!"

"Have you forgotten?" asked my brother "What special thing do we do every year on the day before Christmas?" Then just as if they were back in school, Candi raised her hand excitedly "I know!, I know!" "OK Candi," David said, " tell me what special thing are we going to do today?"

"We are going to make Christmas Boxes!" said Candi with a big smile on her face.

"That's right. I have a list of the three families we selected to make boxes for this year and the names and ages of the children. Ya'll know who these kids are and what they like . So let's get busy so that we are ready to deliver them by nightfall. Any questions?"

Of course there were always questions, and today was no different, what kid doesn't have a million questions. Timidly Charles, who was about 4 at the time, raised his little hand and said, "Daddy why do we make the boxes, how come I gotta give up my toys, I don't wanna, their mine." David leaned over, picked up Charles and put him on his lap. Then he wrapped his arms around him, gave him a squeeze and then looked him straight in the eyes, "Charles, I'm glad you asked that question. Sometimes we forget why we do things and need to be reminded. Every year now for several years we go thru the house looking for things that we don't use anymore, clothes we've outgrown, toys that we've outgrown or don't play with anymore. We bring them into the family room and put them into a big pile. Do you remember?" Charles nodded his head that he remembered, but Chase who was only two just gazed at his father with a confused look because of course he didn't remember any of this because of his tender age. David then picked up Chase and placed him on his other knee and continued his explanation.

"Kids, we make up these boxes for others because we have been blessed with so much, we need to share with those who are not as lucky as we are. Every year at Christmas you are blessed with so many presents under the tree and have so much to play with that you forget about all the toys you already have. So why not give those old toys to someone who will love them as much as you did when you first got them? When we give of ourselves and our possessions to those in need, then we are following in the footsteps of Jesus. For he said, 'If you do it unto the least of these my brethren, you have done it unto me.' Do you want to be like Jesus?" All the children nodded their heads enthusiastically and David continued. "When we give to those in need it makes us feel happy. At this time of year we need to remember that even though Santa Claus comes to our house and leaves you presents, there would be no Santa or presents if Jesus had not been born in a tiny stable in Bethlehem. The birth of Jesus is the reason we have Christmas in the first place. Do ya'all understand?" Four little heads bobbed up and down that they did indeed understand. "So what do ya' think," David said enthusiastically, " can we go on our own treasure hunt ?"

"YES!" resounded through the room.

"OK then everyone go to your rooms and search thru your toys, and find clothes that you have outgrown that you are willing to give away. Then bring them back in here to the family room and put them in a pile here in the middle of the floor. OK then let's begin the treasure hunt. On your mark, *get set*, GO!" The children all ran to their rooms and began to search for hidden treasures. In the mean time David walked over to Vicki and gave her a kiss on the cheek, "While the kids are busy in their rooms, why don't you search our rooms for some gifts for the parents. What d'ya think?"

With a sly grin, Vicki bowed her head and said, "Yes, Master I hear and obey." And with that Vicki moved quickly to the master bedroom and began her search.

"Well Myn," David began, "I guess that leaves you and me and have I got a sweet project for the two of us." Then he put his arm around my shoulders and guided me into the kitchen, "Here's our fortress. From here we will create sweet treats and tasty confections for our benefactors." I began to laugh and David got that silly grin on his face that he always gets when he knows that he has bested his big sister. We donned our aprons, gathered recipe books and spoons, and began to bake cookies and make candy of every type and variety. The aroma of fresh baked cookies filled the house, along with the sounds of children laughing and Christmas carols being sung. Happiness and contentment abounded within the walls of this home and I was totally enveloped in the whole experience of doing for others. When David and I were finished with our tasty treats, the kitchen looked as if a Tennessee tornado had passed through. Bowls were piled in the sink, chocolate chips were scattered here and there on the floor. Bits of flour and stacks of spices lined the kitchen counters. A big floured hand print had appeared on my shoulder and David had flour on his nose and chin. Our aprons looked well used, to say the least. We looked at the kitchen table brimming with all sorts of goodies and we were pleased with our efforts.

"OK Dave," I said, "guess it is time to clean up the kitchen. I'll wash and you can rinse and dry." He agreed. As we cleaned, we talked about the Christmas' we shared together as kids. Pleasant memories filled the room and we both laughed about the Christmas Gene asked if he had to open any more presents, or the time when we all got our first treasure chests. I washed the last few dishes and placed them in the sink to be rinsed. David picked up the sprayer to rinse the dishes, but, rinsed me instead. Then it became just like old times David and I fighting for the sprayer and seeing who could get the other the wettest. I finally managed to turn the water off and David went flying out of the room. I chased him down the hall, determined to give him the tickling of his life, when Vicki stuck her head out of the bedroom door and yelled, "All right you two, no running in the hall. You know better than that." And of course we did, but it didn't make any difference.

I caught up to him in the family room and started to tickle him (he was always the ticklish one), when all four kids came bounding into the room and played dog pile on Aunt Myndy. The episode turned into tickle the kids. Soon the room was filled with laughing children trying to tickle each other and their father as well. I was immune to their tickling because their father and his brothers had spent so much time tickle torturing me when I was young, I was determined not to be ticklish anymore, and to this day I'm not ticklish. When the tickle fest was finished, there were bodies strewn around the floor trying to get their breath and all wearing extremely large smiles. David asked, "OK kids, where are we at ... have you finished your treasure hunt?" Four little heads all nodded yes.

We then looked into the middle of the room and saw a huge pile of toys, clothing and other miscellaneous items. I was amazed at how many things the children were willing to give up for someone else's pleasure. The next task was to separate the toys from the clothing, and to stack the clothes together by size. The kids then made a pile for each person on the list. Any toys or clothing left over were to be donated to a local charity. Vicki brought in rolls of brightly colored wrapping paper, ribbons, tags and tape, and the gifts were gaily wrapped and tagged. No expense was spared to make sure that every present looked perfect, just like they would want to get themselves. Vicki brought out three large boxes she had gotten from the local grocery store and they wrapped the outside of the boxes. With the basic work done we began to pack the boxes, for that we divided into three teams. As the boxes began to fill so did the excitement in the room.

We then turned our attention to the table in the kitchen, laden with the multitude of cookies, candies and breads that had been made earlier. Each team filled up tins and plates with the sweet smelling confections and carefully added them to the already full boxes. And when Chad thought nobody was looking I caught him stuffing Snickerdoodles into his mouth, I'm sure he wasn't the only one taste testing our wares. The final touch was making a card wishing each family a "Merry Christmas from the Christmas Fairy" and then placing a monstrous bow on top. Then we all stood back at gazed at the sight in front of us. I thought what a wonderful idea to share with others what we had so much of. I couldn't image what the faces of the people would be like when we delivered the boxes. Would it be like Bob Cratchit's when old Scrooge showed up with his many parcels for his family, or would it be somewhat more humble. I guess I would have to wait now till after dinner.

Finally the hour had come. Dinner was complete and the dishes had been cleared and everyone was scampering around to get on their coats, hats, gloves and boots on. David cupped his hands to his mouth and said, "Let's load 'em up and move'em out! OK guys, everyone in the car, let's make some magic."

Magic, what kind of magic could he possibly be thinking of. All we were doing was taking three gift laden boxes to some people. What in the world is he talking about ... magic indeed, I thought. But soon found out what kind of magic he was talking about.

In the car everyone was singing Christmas carols together and we were all filled with happiness and mirth. As we approached the first house David turned off the lights of the car, and slowly and silently went just past the front door. David turned around to the group huddled in the back of the car and said, "Shhh, we have to be very quiet . Do you remember what we do now? You have to be as quiet as a church mouse. Put the box at the front door, ring the door bell and run and hide in the bushes so you are not seen. Stay there until they take the box in and close their door. Then you can come back to the car, we will be just around the corner out of sight. We don't want to be discovered, because we don't want anyone to think that they owe us anything. We want them to enjoy the real meaning of Christmas, that in the giving we gain real happiness. It will be our little secret. OK now, which team wants to go first?"

Every hand in the car went up, and David decided that Vicki and Charles would go first. They quietly opened the door and took their precious treasure box to the front door, leaving foot prints in the snow as they went. They rang the door bell and then quickly hid themselves. The porch light went on and the father's face peeked out the front door and looked to see who had rung the bell. Not seeing anyone he started to close the door when he saw the brightly decorated box brimming with packages. His whole face lit up and he called for his family to come see. The children all scampered to the door. When they saw the box, they began to jump up and down and clap their hands. "Can we open it now, can we, can we!" they all said. "First, let's get it inside where it is warm, and you can all help me put these things under the tree. I guess we'll have a Christmas after all. Someone must be watching over us," father said. And he walked out on the porch one more time and surveyed the yard to see if he could catch a glimpse of who might have left the box. Not seeing anyone he went back inside, closed the door and turned off the porch light. That was the Vicki and Charles cue to come back and get in the car. One down, two to go.

As they bounded into the car their faces were beaming, and I wondered how they felt. We had just caught a glimpse of the episode and so didn't get the whole picture. We went to the next house and David and Chad did the same thing. They too bounded back to the car smiling like Cheshire cats. We approached the third home, but this time it was Candi and my turn to deliver the goods. I got butterflies in my stomach as we quietly approached the front door. I set the box down and Candi pushed the doorbell. Then we quickly ran for cover, I managed to get under a bush near the front window. Again the front porch light came on, and just like the other two, the father carefully peered out the front door and looked to see who was there. He then discovered the box sitting next to the door filled with our gifts, but this time instead of calling for his family he just stood there and started to cry. His wife came to the door to see what was wrong and upon seeing the box of goodies she threw her arms around her husband and said joyfully, "God really does hear our prayers. Children come quickly and see what the angels have left us." The children came running to help bring in the box and were so excited to see the brightly colored packages they could hardly contain themselves. I watched as they carried the box in, dropping oranges and candy canes on the floor where the youngest child gathered up the goodies as quickly as she could and made a pile which she eyed with wonder. The father looked once again out the door to see if he could find his benefactors, but not seeing anyone, just looked up to the brightest star in the sky and said, "Thank you God for watching out for my family." He then closed the door and turned out the porch light. I peeked into the window to see an excited family full of thanks about the gifts left on their porch. I looked at the sad little tree in the corner with a few homemade ornaments on it and nothing under its branches and realized that this family had nothing and what we brought to them was truly a box full of treasures. Not simply our unneeded stuff.

As Candi and I hustled to the car, I had a sense of great satisfaction for being able to bring happiness into someone else's life. My heart swelled as did my eyes with tears that the plain and simple things in life can bring so much joy to your soul if you let it. The car was silent, but you could just feel the excitement inside, like a balloon ready to burst from being over filled. It was an awesome feeling and made for a perfect Christmas Eve.

When I reflect now on that Christmas so many years ago, I realize that what my brother's family gave to those folks was hope for a brighter future. That our shepherd really does watch over his flock and leads us to those we can lift up. What I thought was going to be an awful Christmas turned out to be a season of inspiration and love. I had forgotten what a great feeling I had preparing and giving away those boxes without letting anyone know who had left them. My little secret gave me such joy all that year.

Again I looked at the piles of toys strewn all over my floors and decided that this year was going to count for something. We could give something back for all the many blessings we had received that year. I called to the children to come quickly to the family room. They all came scurrying in, pushing and shoving to get to me first. I put my arms around them and looked them straight in the eye and said, "Guess what? Daddy and I have something special for us to do. How would you like to go ... on a treasure hunt ?!"

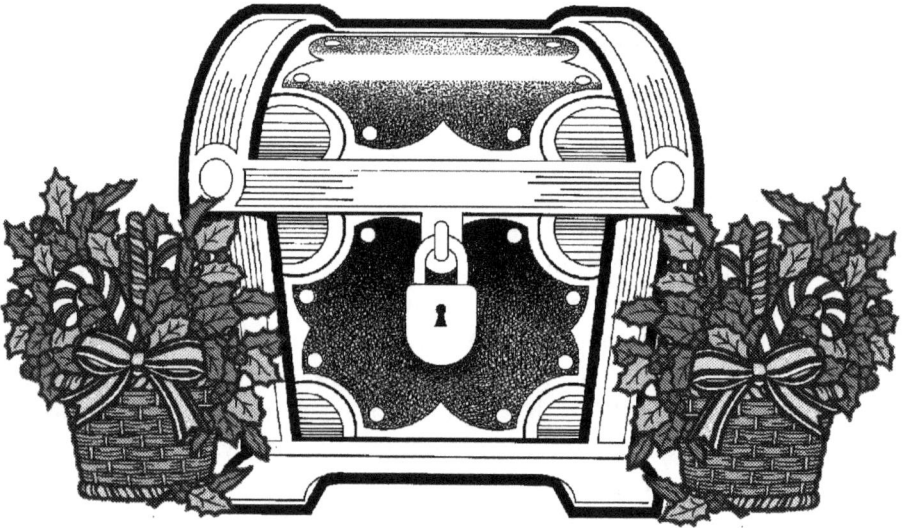

Gift of Love
Gift Giving

USE YOUR IMAGINATION TO CREATE WAYS TO GIVE **GIFTS OF LOVE**. HERE ARE SOME INEXPENSIVE WAYS TO GIVE OF YOURSELF TO OTHERS. FOR ISN'T THAT REALLY THE REASON FOR THE SEASON? BELOW ARE SOME SIMPLE SUGGESTIONS FOR CREATING SOME THOUGHTFUL SURPRISES JUST BEFORE CHRISTMAS, YOU MIGHT EVEN THINK OF SOME YOU LIKE BETTER.

IDEA BARREL:

1. Gift certificates or scrolls can be made using blank white cards or construction paper. Crayons, paints, stickers, ribbons, or picture cutouts can be used to make each one special. On each card offer something special like, good for one kiss, good for one day of baby-sitting, or order a free batch of your favorite cookies. Make booklets of 5 or 6 certificates. Use your imagination, this is a good way to give of yourself.

2. If you have flourishing house plants, give rooted cuttings from your favorites to friends and relatives. After placing them in a pot or jar, wrap a ribbon around the edge and finish with a bow.

3. Give a copy of your favorite recipe to a friend who has always wanted to try it along with the prepared item, on a gift plate or tin.

4. If you have a special talent or accomplishment, make up a gift certificate for a free lesson or a course in ceramics, cooking, sewing, art, language, music, flower arranging, etc.

5. Help decorate the home and fill the refrigerator of an elderly neighbor.

6. Deliver baskets of homemade Christmas goodies decorated with red and green balloons to hospital patients.

7. Play Santa or Mrs. Santa, complete with costume, to a children's hospital ward.

8. Spend Christmas Eve working in a soup kitchen.

9. Instead of giving presents one year, donate to a variety of charities in the name of each friend and family member; suggest they do the same as your gift.

10. Organize a canned food drive at your church or local supermarket.

11. Collect used teddy bears and dolls. Repair and clean them up. Make new clothes for the dolls. Take them to a center for abused women and children or your local police or fire department.

12. Go through your closet and take out all the good used clothes and coats that you no longer wear or are too small for you and put them in a box and take to the local homeless shelter.

13. Donate your services as chauffeur to an otherwise home bound elderly person.

14. Offer an evening of babysitting to someone who can't afford a baby-sitter.

15. Go through your kitchen cupboard and find old mugs that are never used and give them new life by filling it with your favorite variety of hot chocolate or Imitation Russian Tea (see Day 24). Put filling in a baggie, place in mug and add a ribbon, it is ready for gift giving.

16. Make several batches of your favorite cookies. Now stack up a dozen or so and wrap them in plastic wrap to keep fresh, then wrap them in colorful wrapping paper and top with a bow. Deliver them anonymously to your neighbors with a tag that says "For a Good Neighbor".

17. Make a batch of your favorite caramel corn (see Day 13) or butter popcorn and place in candy jars, baskets or cans. Or decorate lunch bags and fill with your special persons favorite popcorn or a mix of popcorns then fold over the top of the bag punch two holes through all four layers and insert a candy cane for a closure. Give to your favorite popcorn lover.

18. Write down a favorite story from your youth. Add photos or drawings to illustrate story. Make color photocopy of it and give it to members of your family.

19. Bake up your favorite type of bread (see Day 5) with your child's help. Wrap it up with a kitchen towel and adorn with ribbon, a sprig of greenery and give to your child's' teacher.

20. Make up a Christmas stockings and fill with candy and small gift items and give to a less fortunate family.

21. Gather a group together and go Christmas caroling in your neighborhood or to a local nursing home or hospice. Don't forget the children or the hot chocolate and cookies when you are done.

22. Remember how you used to toilet paper your friends houses when you were a youth? Change this around and fill their tree with bright red ribbons and ornaments. Make a large Christmas card out of posterboard and write on it "Wishing You and Yours a Merry Christmas! (or Happy Hanukkah)".

23. New Move-in or New Baby in your neighborhood? Fix an entire meal for them and surprise them by showing up early in the afternoon with your goodie basket. Don't forget to add a small wreath or potted plant or a jar of your homemade jelly with your name and telephone number on it as your new neighbor.

24. Take one of your children's favorite drawings and have it framed.

Snickerdoodles

½   cup butter or margarine, softened
½   cup shortening
1½   cups sugar
2   eggs
2¾   cups all purpose flour
2   teaspoons cream of tartar
1   teaspoon soda
¼   teaspoon salt
2   tablespoons sugar
2   teaspoons cinnamon

Heat oven to 400° F. Mix thoroughly butter, shortening, 1½ cups sugar and the eggs. Blend in flour, cream of tartar, soda and salt. Shape dough by rounded teaspoonfuls into balls.

Mix 2 tablespoons sugar and the cinnamon; roll balls in mixture. Place 2 inches apart on ungreased baking sheet. Bake 8 to 10 minutes or until set. Immediately remove from baking sheet.

Makes 6 dozen cookies

VARIATION: Just for fun try experimenting with this recipe a little by hiding different kinds of candies inside the dough (i.e.; would wrap the dough around a chocolate kiss, M&M's, miniature marshmallows, etc.). You can also add a peanut butter cup or a chocolate kiss in the center of the hot cookie and let it melt. Yum! Have fun experimenting.

NOTE: Growing up this had to be my brother David's favorite cookie. Christmas baking was not complete unless we made two batches of Snickerdoodles. One to eat and one to give away.

The Night Before Christmas

Clement C. Moore

TWAS the night before Christmas, when all through the house
Not a creature was stirring, not even a mouse;
The stockings were hung by the chimney with care,
In hopes that St. Nicholas soon would be there;

The children were nestled all snug in their beds,
While visions of sugar-plums danced in their heads;
And mamma in her 'kerchief, and I in my cap,
Had just settled our brains for a long winter's nap,

When out on the lawn there arose such a clatter,
I sprang from the bed to see what was the matter.
Away to the window I flew like a flash,
Tore open the shutters and threw up the sash.

The moon on the breast of the new-fallen snow
Gave the luster of mid-day to objects below,
When, what to my wondering eyes should appear,
But a miniature sleigh, and eight tiny reindeer,

With a little old driver, so lively and quick,
I knew in a moment it must be St. Nick.
More rapid than eagles his coursers they came,
And he whistled, and shouted, and called them by name:

"Now, *Dasher!* now *Dancer,* now, *Prancer* and *Vixen!*
On, *Comet!* on, *Cupid!* on, *Donner!* and *Blitzen!*
To the top of the porch! to the top of the wall!
Now dash away! dash away! dash away all!"

As dry leaves that before the wild hurricane fly,
When they meet with an obstacle, mount to the sky,
So up to the house-top the coursers they flew,
With the sleigh full of toys, and St. Nicholas too.
And then, in a twinkling, I heard on the roof

The prancing and pawing of each little hoof.
As I drew in my head, and was turning around,
Down the chimney St. Nicholas came with a bound.

He was dressed all in fur, from his head to his foot,
And his clothes were all tarnished with ashes and soot;
A bundle of toys he had flung on his back,
And he looked like a peddler just opening his pack.

His eyes—how they twinkled! his dimples how merry!
His cheeks were like roses, his nose like a cherry!
His droll little mouth was drawn up like a bow,
And the beard of his chin was as white as the snow;

The stump of a pipe he held tight in his teeth,
And the smoke it encircled his head like a wreath;
He had a broad face and a little round belly,
That shook, when he laughed, like a bowlful of jelly.

He was chubby and plump, a right jolly old elf,
And I laughed when I saw him, in spite of myself;
A wink of his eye and a twist of his head,
Soon came to know I had nothing to dread.

He spoke not a word, but went straight to his work,
And filled all the stockings; then turned with a jerk,
And laying his finger aside of his nose,
And giving a nod, up the chimney he rose;

He sprang to his sleigh, to his team gave a whistle,
And away they all flew like the down of a thistle.
But I heard him exclaim, ere he drove out of sight,

"Happy Christmas to All, and to All a Good-Night!"

Snowy Scenes
Art Activity

MATERIALS LIST:

> *old shirt*
> *shaving cream**

INSTRUCTIONS:

1. Spray shaving cream* into mounds on kitchen table. Put an old shirt on the kids; they will get it on them.

2. With your hands spread out shaving cream until you have a nice surface to draw on.

3. Now let your children have fun. Draw your favorite snow scenes using your fingers or popsicle sticks. If you don't like what you've just drawn, run your hand over the picture and start again. If the shaving cream starts to dry out or evaporate a little either add a little water or more shaving cream. (The first time I tried this with my 3 year old daughter, she was drawing pictures for over an hour).

4. When your finished, wipe the table with a damp cloth. The table comes remarkably clean and smells fresh.

NOTE: Be sure not to let the kids rub their eyes or mouth, it will sting and definitely not taste good.

*To do this project with small children use vanilla pudding mixed with water. Keep it stiff. Use cereal for snowman eyes and buttons. With this mixture it is okay for the kids to eat the scenery.

Yule Log Cake

Powdered sugar
½   cup all purpose flour
¼   cup cocoa
1   teaspoon baking powder
¼   teaspoon salt
4   eggs, separated (room temperature)
¾   cup sugar
1   teaspoon vanilla
2   tablespoon water

1   can (Ready to Spread) Coconut-Pecan Frosting
1   can (Ready to Spread) Chocolate Fudge Frosting
     candied cherries, quartered to make flowers (optional)

Heat oven to 350°F. Generously grease bottom only of 15x10x1-inch baking pan; line with waxed paper and grease again. Lightly sprinkle clean towel with powdered sugar. Lightly spoon flour into measuring cup; level off. In small bowl, combine flour, coca, baking powder and salt; set aside. In small bowl, beat egg whites until foamy. Gradually add half of sugar, beating continuously until stiff peaks form. Set aside.

In large bowl, beat egg yolks until thick. Add remaining sugar and vanilla; beat until very thick. Stir in water. Gradually add flour mixture to egg yolk mixture. Gently fold in beaten egg whites. Spread batter in greased and lined pan. Bake at 350°F for 14 to 18 minutes or until toothpick inserted in center comes out clean. Loosen edges; immediately invert cake into sugared towel. Remove waxed paper. Starting at shorter end, roll up cake in towel; cool completely on wire rack.

Unroll cooled cake; remove towel. Spread cake with Coconut Pecan Frosting; roll up again, rolling loosely to incorporate filling. Place on serving plate. Frost sides and top of filled cake roll with Chocolate Fudge Frosting. With fork, comb frosting to resemble bark. Garnish with candied cherries which have been quartered and arranged to look like flowers, adding 2 pieces (quartered) of green candied cherries to make leaves.

Makes 10-12 servings

St. Luke 2: 1-20

from the King James Version of The Holy Bible

AND it came to pass in those days, that there went out a decree from Caesar Augustus, that all the world should be taxed. (And this taxing was first made when Cyrenius was governor of Syria.) And all went to be taxed, every one into his own city. And Joseph also went up from Galilee, out of the city of Nazareth, into Judaea, unto the city of David, which is called Bethlehem; (because he was of the house and lineage of David:) to be taxed with Mary his espoused wife, being great with child. And so it was, that, while they were there, the days were accomplished that she should be delivered. And she brought forth her firstborn son, and wrapped him swaddling clothes, and laid him in a manger; because there was no room for them in the inn.

And there were in the same country shepherds abiding in the field, keeping watch over their flock by night. And, lo, the angel of the Lord came upon them, and the glory of the Lord shone round about them: and they were sore afraid. And the angel said unto them, "Fear not: for , behold, I bring you good tidings of great joy, which shall be to all people. For unto you is born this day in the city of David a Saviour, which is Christ the Lord. And this shall be a sign unto you; Ye shall find the babe wrapped in swaddling clothes, lying in a manger. And suddenly there was with the angel a multitude of the heavenly host praising God, and saying, "Glory to God in the highest, and on earth peace, good will toward men."

And it came to pass, as the angels were gone away from them into the heaven, the shepherds said one to another. "Let us now go even unto Bethlehem, and see this thing which is come to pass, which the Lord hath made known unto us." And they came with haste, and found Mary, and Joseph, and the babe lying in a manager. And when they had seen it, they made known abroad the saying which was told them concerning this child. And all they that heard it wondered a those things which were told them by the shepherds. But Mary kept all these things, and pondered them in her heart. And the shepherds returned, glorifying and praising God for all the things that they had heard and seen, as it was told unto them.

The Christmas Carol Game
Family Activity

MATERIALS LIST:

copy of clues   *glue*
scissors   *3x5 index cards*
timer and or watch   *whistle*
candy cane

This is a game to test your knowledge of Christmas music (this includes carols, traditional music as well as new holiday songs). The clues are shown in bold text and the answers are in parenthesis. You will note that the clues are merely the names of each song with a worded twist.

OBJECTIVE: Be the first person to collect three cards. A card is collected by answering correctly the last song on a card.

GAME SETUP: To play the game photocopy the clues below. Cut apart on dotted lines and paste onto 3x5 index cards. There should be three clues/answers on each card. Prepare the cards well in advance and keep hidden until you are ready to play. Identify an individual to be the Clue Master; the one to read the clues and run the timer. Identify an individual to be the Time Keeper; this person should have access to a watch (digital preferred) or some other time keeping device. The Time Keeper needs to be able to alert players to the 10 seconds time play by a short blow on his/her whistle. The purpose of the Time Keeper is to limit players time to answer each clue. (When we played this game originally we used the timer from the *Oodles* game by Milton Bradley). You will also need a candy cane which is used to identify who the current player is. Select first player and give them the candy cane.

DIRECTIONS FOR GAME:

1.   The Clue Master reads the first clue from the first card, starting the timer as they read the clue. (Hint: The Clue Master should read over each card silently before giving them, some of the clues are real tongue twisters and you want to give each player their full time to answer.) The person with the candy cane is the current player and is the current player authorized to answer the question, they may give as many answers as wanted within the 10 second time frame. If

they answer the clue correctly the Clue Master then proceeds to the next clue on the card and the current player again tries to answer the clue correctly. Note the timer needs to be reset for 10 seconds for each clue before it is read. If the ten seconds run out before the current player gives the correct answer then it becomes all play, which means any player can try to answer the clue. All players still only have 10 seconds to answer the clue. The player that answered the clue correctly is the player that receives the next clue and has a chance to answer. If it was the last clue on the card the Clue Master gives the card to the player who answered correctly. If nobody gives the right answer to the last clue on the card, the Clue Master keeps that card. The candy cane is passed onto the next player when no one has answered the clue correctly or a card has been given to a player. Play continues until one player has collected three cards. That player is then dubbed the Christmas Song Master and they get to eat the candy cane. In case of a tie, use the tie breaker question for the parties in question, the player who first answers the question right ... wins.

2. Team Play: A team is two or more players. All regular rules still apply with the exception that any member of the team may answer the clues.

Listen to the Celestial Choir
(Hark the Herald Angels Sing)

O Yuletide Tall woody plant
(O Christmas Tree)

Rapture to the Planet
(Joy to the World)

A dozen times of light between one Yuletide nocturnal
period and the next.
(Twelve Days of Christmas)

Firmament dwellers apprehend by the ear by first person plural
(Angels We Have Heard on High)

The edible part of a tree of the Beech family toasting on a phenomenon of combustion manifested in light
(Chestnuts Roasting on an Open Fire)

Female parental unit observed caressing with the lips gift
bearing Yuletide figure by first person singular
(I saw Mommy Kissing Santa Claus)

Age challenged sleigh driving person is advancing to municipality
(Santa Claus is Coming to Town)

Chilly crystalline precipitation non-female being
(Frosty the Snow Man)

At the Peak of the Domicile
(Up on the House Top)

Duel Noel wish for upper Incisor
(All I want for Christmas is my Two Front Teeth)

**Rudimentary start of mature appearance of
last calendar Holiday**
(It's Beginning to look a lot like Christmas)

Clinking Carillons
(Jingle Bells)

**Junket over naturally occurring surface aquifer
and timberlands**
(Over the River & through the Woods)

Carillons apprehended by ear during December 25th
(I Heard the Bells on Christmas Day)

Toys R Us
(Toyland)

**Move hitherward the entire assembly of
those who are loyal in their belief**
(O Come All Ye Faithful)

Embellish interior passageways
(Deck the Halls)

Vertically challenged adolescent percussionist
(Little Drummer Boy)

**Natal Celebration devoid of color as a
hallucinatory phenomenon for me**
(I'm Dreaming of a White Christmas)

Majestic triplet referred to in the first person plural
(We Three Kings)

Twelve o'clock on a clement night witnessed its arrival
(It Came Upon A Midnight Clear)

Soundless nocturnal period
(Silent Night)

The Yuletide occurrence preceding all others
(The First Noel)

Precious metal musical devices
(Silver Bells)

Omnipotent supreme being who elicits respite to ecstatic distinguished males
(God Rest Ye Merry Gentlemen)

Caribou with vermilion olfactory appendage
(Rudolph the Red Nosed Reindeer)

Allow crystalline formations to descend, Allow crystalline formations to descend, Allow crystalline formations to descend
(Let it Snow, Let it Snow, Let it Snow)

Jovial Yuletide desired for the second person singular or plural by us
(We Wish You a Merry Christmas)

Bipedal traveling through an amazing acreage during the period between December 21st and March 21st
(Walking Through A Winter Wonderland)

TIE BREAKER QUESTION

Exclamatory remark concerning a diminutive municipality in Judea southwest of Jerusalem
(O Little Town of Bethlehem)

Christmas Eve Buffet

Assorted Meats & Cheeses
Cornmeal Rolls • 24 Hour Salad
Tennessee BBQ Sausage Pennies
Ham Dip with assorted fresh vegetables & crackers
Cherry Crisp • Creme Puffs
Spiced Apprange Punch

Cornmeal Rolls

1¾ cups water	⅓ cup cornmeal
¼ cup sugar	3 tablespoons salt
½ cup warm water (110°- 115° F.)	
2 packages active dry yeast	
2 eggs	
5½ cups all purpose flour	
melted butter or margarine	
additional cornmeal	

In a saucepan, combine 1¾ cups water, cornmeal, sugar, oil and salt. Cook and stir over medium heat until mixture boils, about 9 - 11 minutes. Cool at room temperature to 120° - 130° F. Place in a mixing bowl. Dissolve yeast in 1/2 cup warm water (110° to 115° F) add to cornmeal mixture. Add eggs and mix well. Add enough flour to make a soft dough. Turn onto a floured board; knead until smooth and elastic about 6-8 minutes. Place in a greased bowl, turning once to grease top. Cover and let rise in a warm place until doubled, about 45 to 60 minutes.* Punch dough down. Shape into 24 balls. Place on greased baking sheets; brush with butter and sprinkle with cornmeal. Let rise, uncover, until doubled, about 30 minutes. Bake at 375° F. for 18-20 minutes or until golden brown. Immediately remove from pan; serve warm.

Makes 2 dozen rolls

*To speed up the rising time, preheat oven to 125° F. then turn off the oven. Place bowl in warm oven. Dough will be ready to punch down and shape in about 20 - 30 minutes, thereby cutting your rising time in half.

Overnight Salad

"This is the absolute best salad I have ever eaten, and I don't particularly like peas." Judy Bowden - Kitchen Tester

1	head lettuce, torn
½	cup celery, chopped
½	cup green pepper, diced
1	small onion, diced
1	10 ounce package frozen peas, thawed
1	8 ounce can water chestnuts, sliced
1	cup mayonnaise
1	cup cheddar cheese, shredded
6	slices bacon, fried, crumbled

Layer vegetables in the following order: Lettuce, celery, green pepper, onion, peas and water chestnuts. Spread mayonnaise over top sealing all edges. Cover with plastic wrap and refrigerate for 24 hours. Sprinkle cheese and bacon over the top. Toss from the bottom before serving

Makes 12 servings

Holiday Potatoes

"The best I ever had." Erin Potter - Kitchen Tester

8	medium potatoes, cooked and shredded
½	cup butter or margarine
2	cans cream of chicken soup
1	pint sour cream
1½	cup sharp cheddar cheese
6	green onions, chopped
	cornflakes

Preheat oven to 350° F.. Cook in saucepan over low heat, butter, soup, sour cream, cheese and onions until cheese melts. In a 9x13 inch pan grate half the potatoes, then pour 1/3 of the sauce over potatoes and repeat process ending with sauce. Crumble up corn flakes and place on top. Bake until lightly browned and cheese is melted about 20 minutes.

Makes 8-12 servings

Tennessee BBQ Sausage Pennies

"Simple, but oh so tasty!" Jeremy Potter - Kitchen Tester

| 1 | pound Kelbasa Sausage | 1 | bottle BBQ sauce |

Slice sausage into ½ thick circles. Pour BBQ sauce into a medium sized pot and warm over medium heat. Add sausage pennies and continue to cook until sausage is completely warmed.

Makes 12 servings

Ham Dip

1	8 ounce package cream cheese
1	package 2.5 ounce wafer thin smoked ham
½	small onion
2	tablespoons milk
⅛	teaspoon pepper

In food processor mince onion and ham, then put in small bowl. Cut cream cheese into cubes and place in food processor along with milk and pepper. Process until cream cheese is smooth. Blend cream cheese mix with onion and ham, until thoroughly mixed. The mix should be soft and creamy enough to use as a dip. If it is still stiff add a few more drops of milk until you achieve the desired consistency. Chill at least one hour before serving. Serve with assorted vegetables, crackers, chips or spread on bread.

VARIATION: If you would prefer to have a cheese ball reduce the amount of milk to 1 teaspoon. With a large wooden spoon mix in the ham and onion, and form into a ball. Then roll ball into chopped pecans. Will make one small cheese ball. Note: try the other varieties of packaged meats for a flavor change (i.e.; smoked beef, peppered beef, pastrami, etc.)

Cherry Crisp

1   can (21 ounce) cherry pie filling
⅔   cup brown sugar packed
½   cup all purpose flour
½   cup oats
¾   teaspoon cinnamon
¾   teaspoon nutmeg
⅓   cup butter or margarine, softened

Preheat oven to 375° F. Grease square pan, 8x8x2 inches. Place cherry pie filling in bottom of pan. Mix remaining ingredients thoroughly. Sprinkle over cherries.

Bake 30 minutes or until topping is golden brown. Serve warm and, if desired, with whipped cream or ice cream.

Makes 6 Servings

Suggestions: To make Apple Crisp instead; use 4 cups sliced pared tart apples (about 4 medium).

Creme Puffs

1   cup water
½   cup butter or margarine
1   cup all purpose flour
4   eggs
       Vanilla Pudding or sweetened whipped cream
       Powdered sugar

Preheat oven to 400° F. Heat water and butter to rolling boil. Stir in flour. Stir vigorously over low heat about 1 minute or until mixture forms a ball. Remove from heat. Beat in eggs, all at one time; continue beating until smooth. Drop dough by scant 1/4 cupfuls 3 inches apart onto ungreased baking sheet.

Bake 35 to 40 minutes or until puffed and golden. Cool away from draft. Cut off tops. Pull out any filaments of soft dough. Carefully fill puffs with pudding. Replace tops; dust with powdered sugar. Refrigerate until serving time.

Makes 12 Creme Puffs

Suggestions: Any flavor of pudding may be used or for fun put a scoop of peppermint ice cream inside and drizzle the top with chocolate syrup.

Spiced Apprange Punch

Not too Sweet, just enough spices to make it interesting

1   64 ounce bottle Apple Juice or Cider
¾   cup Imitation Russian Tea Mix (see below)
½   gallon water
2   2 liter bottle of Ginger Ale

Mix Imitation Russian Tea Mix with 64 ounces (½ gallon) of water and chill. To make one punch bowl full combine half a bottle of apple juice, and 32 ounces of imitation Russian Tea Mix and 1 bottle of ginger ale into large punch bowl. You can make two punch bowls with this recipe. Serve with ice.

Makes 60 (6 ounce cup) servings

VARIATION: Try serving this punch hot, just omit the ginger ale. It is very fragrant and warming. I also like to make up some extra Imitation Russian Tea Mix and freeze it in a bundt pan and then float it in the punch bowl. Or freeze the Imitation Russian Tea Mix until it is slushy then mix the other ingredients together in punch bowl. Anyway you make it, this is a great unexpectedly good punch.

Imitation Russian Tea

2   cups powdered orange drink mix
1   cup presweetened powdered lemonade mix
1   cup sugar
1   teaspoon cinnamon
½   teaspoon ground cloves

Combine all ingredients in a medium bowl. Mix well. Put in a 1 quart airtight container. Label and keep in a cool dry place. To mix add 2 - 3 teaspoons of mix to 1 cup hot water. Stir to dissolve. Makes 1 serving. For a group add 1⅓ cup mix to a gallon of water. Serve hot or cold.

Christmas Day

BREAKFAST

OVERNIGHT EGGNOG FRENCH TOAST
ORANGE SLICES SPRINKLED WITH SUGAR
HOT CHOCOLATE

Overnight Eggnog French Toast

5	eggs	1½	cups half-and-half or milk
¼	cup sugar	¼	teaspoon nutmeg
1	teaspoons vanilla	¾	teaspoons rum extract
12	3/4 inch thick slices		French bread
	Powdered sugar		jam, jelly, syrup (optional)

Grease a 15x10x1 inch baking pan. In large bowl, combine eggs, half and half, sugar, nutmeg, vanilla and rum extract; beat until well blended. Arrange bread slices in greased baking pans. Pour egg mixture over bread in pans. Lift and move bread slices until all egg mixture is absorbed. Cover with foil; refrigerate overnight or freeze up to one week.

Heat oven to 500° F. Remove bread slices from refrigerator or freezer (do not thaw); remove foil. Bake 1 pan at 500° F. for 15 minutes or until golden brown. Sprinkle with powdered sugar.

Makes 12 slices

VARIATION: I find that if I am feeling really lazy that a half gallon of really good store bought eggnog will do almost as good as the recipe above.

NOTE: This is a great recipe to make the night before so that you don't have to think about cooking breakfast on Christmas morning.

Rejoice... It's Christmas

CHRISTMAS FEAST

Turkey • Sausage Cornbread Dressing
Mashed Potatoes/ Gravy • Green Beans • Corn
Shrimp Coleslaw • Mandarin Orange Delight
Angel Biscuits & Butter • Cranberry Sauce
Angel Food Supreme

Sausage Cornbread Dressing

1	pound bulk pork sausage, mild	1	cup onion, chopped
1	cup celery, chopped	2	teaspoons sage
½	teaspoon thyme	½	teaspoon pepper
½	cup chopped parsley	5	cups crumbled bread crumbs
5	cups crumbled cornbread crumbs	1	cup pecans, coarsely chopped (optional)

Preheat oven to 325° F. Grease a 9x13x2 inch baking pan. Cook sausage, onion and celery in skillet until sausage is brown and vegetables are tender. In large mixing bowl, combine sausage and vegetable mixture with remaining ingredients. Stir gently. Spoon into prepared baking dish. Bake 45-50 minutes or until golden brown.

Makes 10-12 servings

Suggestions: For a little bit of variety add 2 cups chopped Granny Smith apples, unpeeled. This dressing may also be placed in the cavity of the turkey and baked. I think that it adds wonderful seasonings to the turkey.

Shrimp Coleslaw

1	small head cabbage, shredded
2	carrots, shredded
1	green pepper, diced
1	large tomato, diced
1	can baby shrimp, drained
½	cup salad dressing
¼	cup apple cider vinegar
3	tablespoons sugar (more if you like a sweeter slaw)
	salt & pepper to taste

Shred cabbage and carrots and place into medium sized bowl.
Add diced green pepper, tomato and the drained shrimp. Mix
salad dressing, vinegar and sugar together then pour over mix until
blended. Salt and pepper to taste.

Makes 8-10 servings

Mandarin Orange Delight

"This salad was so tasty. It was light and cleansed the palate"
Laurie Grigley - Kitchen Tester

1	6 ounce package orange gelatin
2½	cups boiling water
1	(13 ounce) can crushed pineapple, undrained
1	(6 ounce) can frozen orange juice
2	cans mandarin oranges, drained
1	package instant lemon pudding
1	cup cold milk
2	cups whipped topping

Dissolve orange gelatin in boiling water. Add pineapple and can of frozen orange juice and chill until partially set. Add drained cans of mandarin oranges and pour into a 9x13x2 baking dish and chill until firm.

In another bowl mix pudding and milk until smooth, then fold in whipped topping. Spread pudding mix over gelatin. Chill. Cut into squares and serve.

Makes 12 servings

Angel Biscuits

"My family is in love with this recipe. And it was so fast and easy to make"
Lisa Potter - Kitchen Tester

5	cups flour
¼	cup sugar
1	tablespoon baking powder
1	teaspoon salt
1	cup shortening
1	package dry yeast
2	tablespoons warm water
2	cup buttermilk
½	cup butter, softened or melted

Preheat oven to 400° F. Combine dry ingredients. Cut in shortening until mixture is like coarse meal. Dissolve yeast in water. Stir yeast mixture and buttermilk into flour mixture, mix well. Turn dough out on floured board. Roll 1/4 inch thick rectangle. Spread evenly with butter. Fold dough in half. Cut into 2 inch squares. Place on greased baking sheet. Bake for 15 minutes.

Makes 2 dozen rolls

Angel Food Supreme

1   Angel Food Cake
3   cups chilled whipping cream
1½   cups confectioner's sugar
¾   cup cocoa
⅔   cup toasted slivered almonds

Place cake upside down; slice off entire top of cake about 1 inch down and set aside. Make cuts down into cake 1 inch from outer edge and 1 inch from edge of hole, leaving substantial "walls" on each side. With a spoon carefully remove cake between the cuts, being careful to leave a base of cake on bottom 1 inch thick. Place cake on serving plate.

In a chilled bowl, beat whipping cream, confectioner's sugar and cocoa until stiff. Fold in ⅓ cup toasted slivered almonds into half the whipped cream mixture; now spoon into cake cavity. Press mixture firmly into cavity to avoid "holes" in cut slices. Replace top of cake and press gently.

Frost entire cake with remaining whipped cream mixture. Sprinkle with ⅓ cup toasted slivered almonds. Chill at least 4 hours or until set.

Makes 12 -16 Servings

Suggestions: For a lighter version omit the cocoa and almonds and add to half of the whipped cream mixture 3 tablespoons strawberry gelatin and 1 cup sliced strawberries. With remaining whipped cream mixture frost cake then garnish cake with additional strawberries.

Note: When I was growing up any cake made for Christmas Day was called "Baby Jesus's Birthday Cake". It was the tradition to put one candle on the cake and sing happy birthday to baby Jesus and then everyone blow out the candle. I make this particular cake because it is light on the palate and my stomach after everything else I have eaten today. It truly is heavenly.

Index

Subject Index

Stories & Poems

Activities

Recipes

ACKNOWLEDGMENTS

Anderson, Hans Christian: *The Fir Tree*; translated from Danish by Jean Hersholt ©1942 by Limited Editions Club, Inc.

Butterworth, MyLinda: "A Sweet Reminder" previously called "The Christmas Candy Cane," 1997; Day to Day Enterprises

Church, Francis: *Yes Virginia, There is a Santa Claus*; New York Sun, September 21, 1897

Day, Linda S.: *Handsy Reindeer T-Shirt, Glitter Snow Globe, Christmas Ornaments for Birds, Santa Jar or Wise Man Jar* are from *The Teacher's Craft File*; ©1972 Robert and Robert O. Day and ©1997 Day to Day Enterprises

Day, Robert O.: *Poems for Christmas (Hurray! Hurray! for Christmas Day; Christmas is Coming-Santa's Getting Fat; Making Cookies; Wrapped Up Presents; Merry Christmas!!!)* from the script *Christmas Is ... ;* ©1991 Day to Day Enterprises

Day, Robert O.: *The Bear Who Couldn't Sleep* ©1975 from *Nursery Rhymes and Fairy Tales X*

Author Unknown: "Letter of Thanks"

Field, Eugene: "Jest 'Fore Christmas;" from *Poems of Eugene Field*; 1910, by Julia Sutherland Field; published by Charles Scribner's Sons

Dodge, Mary Mapes: *The Festival of St. Nicholas (*from *Hans Brinker or the Silver Skates), 1865*

Kingsley, Florence, M., "The Star," taken from the book *Christmas Tales and Legends*, 1916, Megis Publishing Co., Indianapolis, Indiana.

Moore, Clement C.: *The Night Before Christmas;* written in 1823

CONTRIBUTORS

Special thanks to Robert O. Day for the use of his stories: "A Lump of Coal for Christmas," "An Adventure Stick for Christmas,"and "The Fourth Wiseman,"

Special thanks to Linda S. Day for the use of her story "The Legend of the Christmas Robin" and "Dad, Do I Hafta?", .

While every effort has been made to secure permission, it has in a few cases proved impossible to trace the author or his executor. If any copyright holder not here acknowledged will contact the publishers, corrections will be made in future editions.

The publishers would like to thank Linda S. Day for her many illustrations scattered throughout this book,

ABOUT THE AUTHOR

When asked where she is from, MyLinda, generally answers, "What year?" MyLinda Butterworth claims she is no army brat but an education brat. Moving from university to university while her father worked for his higher education. MyLinda is the eldest of eight children, which can explain why she needed all those homemaking skills of cooking, sewing and crafting she learned as a youth.

A graduate of Brigham Young University with a degree in Theatre Education, she was prepared to spark the imagination of Junior High and High School students, but opted to help her husband Mike achieve his university education. During that time MyLinda became an award winning costume designer and spent a great deal of time acting, directing and costume designing for a variety of professional and community theatres from Tennessee, Idaho, Arizona and Florida. She is a member of the group StoryMasters™.

The majority of her time now is spent raising their children, Nicole and Sean, in the heart of Florida. MyLinda is an award winning author and shares her talents teaching middle school students what being an author is all about. She is the author of four books.